T̶ ̶ ̶ ̶ of Revelation . . .

★

Can mankind achieve lasting peace on earth? What is the hope for Soviet-American relations? What can solve racial tension in our society? Edgar Cayce perceived the answers to these questions and more in the Universal pattern—a cosmic energy that revealed new beginnings, new hopes, and new challenges. In this illuminating book Mary Ellen Carter documents how hundreds of Edgar Cayce's specific predictions for the future have—and continue to—come startlingly true: from domestic events to international political affairs to scientific advances and individual life stories. Complete with dozens of detailed Life Readings, EDGAR CAYCE ON PROPHECY is a timeless guide to the vast, untapped power of spiritual and psychic illumination and a book that can show you how to use that power for better living now.

☆ ☆ ☆

EDGAR CAYCE
ON
PROPHECY

Published By

WARNER BOOKS

EDGAR CAYCE
ON
PROPHECY

BY MARY ELLEN CARTER

UNDER THE EDITORSHIP OF

HUGH LYNN CAYCE

Director, Association for Research and Enlightenment

WARNER BOOKS

A Warner Communications Company

WARNER BOOKS EDITION

Portions of the chapter "Atlantis Rising?" were published in 1960 in *Orion*
Magazine under the title "Is Atlantis Rising Once More?"

Grateful acknowledgement is made to Dr. Webb Garrison for permission to
quote from *Strange Bonds Between Animals and Men* (Copyright © 1955,
1956, 1957, 1959 by Webb B. Garrison) and to Doubleday & Company, Inc.
for permission to quote from *Man in Time* by J. B. Priestley (Copyright ©
1964 by Aldus Books Ltd., London) and *Aztecs in Mexico* by George C.
Vaillant (Copyright © 1941, 1962 by Doubleday & Company, Inc.).

Cover design by Frank Urrutia

Warner Books, Inc.
666 Fifth Avenue
New York, N.Y. 10103

Ⓦ A Warner Communications Company

Printed in the United States of America

First Warner Books Printing: June, 1968

Reissued: September, 1988

30   29   28   27

CONTENTS

This book is dedicated to
all who are helping make the way clear and passable
for the New Age.

—M. E. C.

Introduction

WHO WAS EDGAR CAYCE?

The eight books which have been written about him have totaled more than a million in sales, and more than ten other books have devoted sections to his life and talents. He has been featured in dozens of magazines and hundreds of newspaper articles dating from 1900 to the present. What was so unique about him?

It depends on whose eyes you look at him through. A goodly number of his contemporaries knew the "waking" Edgar Cayce as a gifted professional photographer. Another cross section (predominantly children) admired him as a warm and friendly Sunday School teacher. His own family knew him as a wonderful husband and father.

The "sleeping" Edgar Cayce was an entirely different figure; a psychic known to thousands of people, in all walks of life, who had cause to be grateful for his help; indeed, many of them believe that he alone had either saved or changed their lives when all seemed lost. The "sleeping" Edgar Cayce was a medical diagnostician, a prophet, and a devoted protagonist of Bible lore.

In June 1954, the University of Chicago held him in sufficient respect to accept a Ph.D. thesis based on a study of his life and work: in this thesis the graduate referred to him as a "religious seer." In June of that same year, the children's comic book *House of Mystery* bestowed on him the impressive title of "America's Most Mysterious Man!"

Even as a child on a farm near Hopkinsville, Kentucky, where he was born on March 18, 1877, Edgar Cayce displayed powers of perception which seemed to extend beyond the normal range of the five senses. At the age of six or seven he told his parents that he was able to see and talk to "visions," sometimes of relatives who had recently died. His parents attributed this to the overactive imagination of a lonely child who had been influenced by the dramatic language of the revival meetings which were popular in that section of the country. Later, by sleeping with his head on his schoolbooks, he developed some form of photographic memory which helped him advance rapidly in the country school. This faded, however, and Edgar was only able to complete his seventh grade before he had to seek his own place in the world.

By twenty-one he had become the salesman for a wholesale stationery company. At this time he developed a gradual paralysis of the throat muscles, which threatened the loss of his voice. When doctors were unable to find a physical cause for these conditions, hypnosis was tried, but failed to have any permanent effect.

As a last resort, Edgar asked a friend to help him re-enter the same kind of hypnotic sleep that had enabled him to memorize his schoolbooks as a child. His friend gave him the necessary suggestion, and once he was in self-induced trance, Edgar came to grips with his own problem. He recommended medication and manipulative therapy which successfully restored his voice and repaired his system.

A group of physicians from Hopkinsville and Bowling Green, Kentucky, took advantage of his unique talent to diagnose their own patients. They soon discovered that Cayce only needed to be given the name and address of the patient, wherever he was, and was then able to "tune in" telepathically on that individual's mind and body as easily as if they were both in the same room. He needed, and was given, no other information regarding any patient.

One of the young M.D.'s, Dr. Wesley Ketchum, submitted a report on this unorthodox procedure to a clinical research society in Boston. On October 9, 1910, *The New York Times* carried two pages of headlines and pictures. From that day on, invalids from all over the country sought the "wonder man's" help.

When Edgar Cayce died on January 3, 1945, in Virginia Beach, Virginia, he left well over fourteen thousand documented stenographic records of the telepathic-clairvoyant statements he had given for more than eight thousand different people over a period of forty-three years. These typewritten documents are referred to as "readings."

These readings constitute one of the largest and most impressive records of psychic perception ever to emanate from a single individual. Together with their relevant records, correspondence and reports, they have been cross-indexed under thousands of subject-headings and placed at the disposal of psychologists, students, writers and investigators who come in increasing numbers to examine them.

A foundation known as the A.R.E. (The Association for Research and Enlightenment, Inc., P.O. Box 595, Virginia Beach, Virginia, 23451) was founded in 1932 to preserve these readings. As an open-membership research society, it continues to index and catalogue the information, initiate investigation and experiments, and promote conferences, seminars and lectures. Until now its published findings have been made available to its members through its own publishing facilities.

Now Paperback Library has made it possible to present a series of popular volumes dealing with those subjects from the Edgar Cayce readings most likely to appeal to public interest.

In this volume Mary Ellen Carter has traced many fascinating threads of prophecy through the complicated tapestry of the thousands of individual readings. Dramatic personal prophecies are in contrast with the world prophecies whose validity is attested daily by our newspaper headlines. Though Edgar Cayce has been dead for twenty-three years, his readings seem very much alive as we examine his statements which have come to pass as well as those describing incidents which lie just ahead.

Mrs. Carter's examination of the major theories on time in the light of the Edgar Cayce readings will stimulate your thinking. She is a good reporter whose book will raise many questions for you, but also answer many which have been suggested by Edgar Cayce's strange prophetic capacities.

—Hugh Lynn Cayce

I

PROPHET OF THE NEW AGE

Edgar Cayce was a prophet of the New Age.

It has also been called the "Great Dispensation," the "Age of Understanding" as he called it; "The Day of the Lord."

It might also be called "the end of the world as we know it."

Thinking about man's history on earth as compared with what the prophets of the past have held up to us as the ideal; considering man's present weariness with wars, degradation, starvation, and the meaningless treadmill that is our lot, maybe this is a pretty good thing.

Looking through our most optimistic shade of rose-colored glasses, we think of the many changes that have already taken place in recent years which have made life better for mankind. The changes of which Edgar Cayce spoke were to be on all levels, including international relationships, science, social conditions, spiritual growth, and man's knowledge of his mind and his inner being. In all this, we find, was a clear sound of the ringing bell of hope, and not of doom. We face a glorious age of expansion and growth because "dispensation" means "special exemption"—"release from obligation." Not that we're worth it, but that God is good.

During his lifetime, Edgar Cayce previsioned the vicissitudes of the Great Depression, pointing out its reasons and its end. He warned of America's entrance into World War II unless she prayed and acted as she prayed. He foretold the New Age Dispensation, which he said would come when "those who are His" have made the way passable and man's history is "folded up."

He was a world prophet, speaking for all the nations, for ancient nations long forgotten by man, and for future centuries hence. He spoke in terms of the long view, in which he himself had been a prophet in at least one past life, and

10

foretold that he would return again in 2100 A.D., remembering his identity as Edgar Cayce!

In January, 1945, Edgar Cayce stepped through "God's other door," as he had often called death, and in eight months, World War II was ended. It seemed the end of an epoch during which he had lived to bring what many have taken to be an unmistakable message of God's love to the world during its worst trials in modern times, and from then on, his message was enough to carry us into the millenium.

As we look back twenty-three years later, we see that man had then needed a prophet and that Cayce said what had to be said, just in time!

Like prophetic passages of the Bible, Cayce's forecasts could become a relic of the past which generations of the future might remember as a curiosity and a strange myth of the twentieth century. Or they could serve to be a source of hope to generations wiser than we.

Unlike most prophets, he spoke in a self-imposed hypnotic trance and did not know what he had said until he returned to consciousness. He depended all his life on others to record and evaluate what he brought forth. It was left to others to present his work to the world, or to forget it.

The readings state in one place that, like Cayce, Ezekiel had a secretary or scribe to take down his utterances.

Also, like Ezekiel, he spoke forcefully of our social ills. He predicted the present race riots and labor troubles as inevitable unless regard was given the underprivileged and disadvantaged. For too long, the social and economic sins of America have been covered up, as in the days of that ancient Hebrew seer, when God likened the hidden evils of Jerusalem to a wall that had been "daubed with whitewash."

If you had compared Edgar Cayce with Ezekiel to his face, he would probably had laughed. His self image was not such that he ranked himself with the major prophets, nor even called himself a minor one. He was a southern Presbyterian Sunday School teacher, a photographer by profession. He was a family man. And then, there was this matter of being psychic. He had a kind of wonder about it all, like everybody else. He was never able to hear himself say all these wonderful, frightening, joyous, terrible, crazy un-Presbyterianlike things recorded by his secretary, whose accuracy his wife confirmed.

By all other psychics of this age, however, he is acknowledged generally to be the greatest among them. In a public talk given in July, 1967, to a Virginia Beach audience, the beautiful prophetess Jeane Dixon said of him, "Edgar Cayce is the expert." She had been asked about predictions she had made regarding many earth changes in the future, which agree with those Cayce made.

He said that he would return in 1998 as a world liberator if he so desired, to help bring about the New Age. "Is it not fitting then that these [old souls] must return?" states this message for Edgar Cayce himself, "as this priest may develop himself to be in that position to be in the capacity of a *liberator* of the world in its relationships to individuals in these periods to come; for he must enter again at that period, or in 1998."

Furthermore, this will also be a time of liberation for Cayce: "When the day of the earth, as earthy, is fulfilled in Him," states Reading 254-83, "this body, Edgar Cayce, shall be rejuvenated, shall be purged, shall be made free."

In the parlance of reincarnation, this doubtless means that he will be freed from the need to reincarnate again. This is possible, say the readings, for any soul who is willing to live as close to spiritual law as did Edgar Cayce.

Following his next incarnation in 1998, however, he will return at least once more by his own volition, if his prophetic dream of being born again in 2100 A.D. is true!

In this dream, he had been born in the year 2100 in Nebraska, and as a child, told his elders that he had been Edgar Cayce in the early twentieth century. The scientists who investigated him were quite bald, and wore long beards and thick glasses.

He recalled his former home states of Alabama, New York, and Virginia. He journeyed with the scientists on their visit to these places, traveling in a long, cigar-shaped metal ship which moved at high speeds through the air.

On this venture he saw that New York had been destroyed and was being rebuilt. Alabama was partly under water, and Norfolk, Virginia was now an immense seaport. Industries were scattered over the country instead of being

12

centralized in cities. Houses were of glass. Many records were discovered proving that Edgar Cayce had lived when he did. The group returned to Nebraska, now America's west coast!

The world was at a low ebb in its history in 1936 when he had this dream, and it was also a personally difficult time for Edgar Cayce. He, his wife Gertrude, and his secretary, Gladys Davis, had just gone through the humiliating experience of being arrested in Detroit for practicing medicine without a license. The court trial ended in their favor, but it had come after months of uncertainty, and as a result, Cayce had suffered in mind and in body.

He dreamed this account of the future the night following the trial. Later, he obtained an interpretation through a reading which assured him that the dream had been for his "understanding that though the moment may appear dark . . . though there may be periods of the misinterpreting of purposes, even these will be turned into that which will be the very proof itself in the experiences of the entity and those whom the entity might . . . help. . . .

"Though the very heavens fall, though the earth shall be changed, though the heavens shall pass, the premises in Him are sure and will stand—as in that day—as the proof of thy activity in the lives and hearts of thy fellow man . . . .

"For indeed and in truth ye know, 'as ye do it unto thy fellowman, ye do it unto thy God, to thyself.' For with self effaced, God may indeed glorify thee and make thee stand as one who is called for a purpose in thy dealings, in thy relationships with thy fellowman. Be not unmindful that He is nigh unto thee in every trial, in every temptation, and hath not willed that thou shouldst perish. Make thy will, then, one with His. Be not afraid. . . ."

As one might suspect, he also had some rather unusual experiences while in the waking state. He lived as a child in Hopkinsville, Kentucky, the life of a typical farm boy. At twelve, he became very religious and spent many hours reading the Bible and praying. One evening after he had gone to bed, he awoke to find his room full of light.

"I thought that my mother had entered the room with a lamp," he told friends years later. Then he realized that the figure which he saw was not that of his mother!

"I heard a voice speaking to me, and was told that a

13

power was going to be given me to help others if I used it properly.

"The next day, I found that by losing consciousness, as if in sleep, after reading or hearing read a lesson, I could remember it all when I awoke."

After this, Cayce advanced rapidly in school. After the seventh grade, he had to quit his formal education and go to work however.

He gave his first reading for himself at twenty-one to find out how he might regain his voice, which he had lost a year before. The reading was his first psychic diagnosis, describing "a congestion in the area of the voice box." The suggestion was given that it could be cured by increasing the circulation in that area. He regained his voice at once.

When news spread of this, people came to him for readings. Newspaper publicity followed. When he was thirty-three, Dr. W. H. Ketchum became interested in him and cooperated with him in diagnosing and curing ailments, for many readings required the skills of a physician to carry out the suggested treatments.

In a speech to a Greek letter fraternity in Pasadena, California, Dr. Ketchum told of his investigation of Cayce. "My subject simply lies down and folds his arms, and by autosuggestion goes to sleep," he began. "While in this sleep, which to all intents and purposes is a natural sleep, his objective mind is completely inactive and only his subjective is working. . . ."

Typical headlines of the earliest newspaper accounts stated "Illiterate Man Becomes a Doctor When Hypnotized" (*New York Times,* October 9, 1910). According to a note in the files, the first record of Cayce's early work was actually made before 1910, but that year seems to be the beginning of his public service as a psychic.

He had learned photography and was anxious to succeed in that profession and to live a normal life. His marriage and the arrival of two boys certainly were reason enough for him to want a stable and secure life for himself and his family. His mysterious ability to help people, which had come to him just as the strange lady with the light had promised, was a wonderful gift. But he found it took much time from his career and family.

14

But as the lady had prophesied, he was to spend a lifetime using his gift for the good of others. As his work spread, the A.R.E. was told that "the day will arise in thine experience . . . of this group who seek, of those present, when they will see, will hear it sounded about the earth . . . ."

This has come to pass, for Cayce and this work have been the subject of books and articles which have indeed "sounded" about the earth. First there was *There Is a River,* the endearing—and enduring—biography of Cayce by his friend, the late Tom Sugrue, published in 1942. Others followed, and at present, Jess Stearn's, *Edgar Cayce: The Sleeping Prophet,* has been a best seller for the past year. Since its publication, interest in and knowledge of Cayce's life and legacy of fourteen thousand readings has mounted. Membership in the Association has tripled and inquiries are swamping the A.R.E. offices. People who never heard of Cayce before 1967 are reading of him, talking about him, and speculating over the many new ideas his life represents.

Foremost among these, of course, is reincarnation. "I don't know whether I believe in it or not," a housewife told me after reading about Cayce recently. "But it's an interesting idea."

There are many such "interesting ideas" in the files which are awaiting perusal of the kind of scholars and researchers—and just plain folk—who insist on leaving no stone unturned in the search for the answers to many questions.

Cayce wrote to a friend in July, 1926: "Of course, don't everybody agree with what the readings say—won't everybody try them all out, and under the circumstances and conditions, I wouldn't blame you one bit . . . ."

He had a very realistic outlook regarding his gift. He was as much in the dark as anybody when he opened his eyes after a reading! But he had also the gift of faith which anyone can have through prayer, reading the Bible, and doing the right thing, day by day. This was all he asked of himself and others. But he knew also how much patience this daily regime took.

He received letters from people for whom he had given

15

readings, attesting to the rewards they had brought. A friend who had lost his job wrote, "When I look at these readings that have been given me for health, life, and work and see how they come jamb up to the line, I am made to know that they cannot be doubted. . . ."

Cayce wrote him, "Don't make plans too far ahead . . . That it [adversity] has taken you almost over the fire, with just seared threads holding you off, is not in condemnation—rather that you might be better acquainted [with God] for we must oft remember that 'though He were the Son, yet learned He obedience through the things which He suffered.' "

This man must have had a prophetic bent, himself, for he replied, "Where a man, country, nation or any organization works and keeps the Will of the Father, no power is greater than He. So I fully believe this work is just being born and will grow to be a worldwide thing, and much quicker than any expect. Why? Because truth and results is what counts, and no arguments can retard it."

The range of universal concepts to which prophecy of this high order was applied was as wide as the mind of man can stretch. It embraced man's deepest yearning to know what lies beyond himself, and beyond the farthest star. It accommodated itself to man's most trivial concerns—one woman asked where she might locate her lost emeralds. In a word, it reflected man himself, which is perhaps what made it all so wonderful.

Specifically, many events of world significance were foretold, including major earth changes in the near future. In the realm of archeology, fascinating forecasts were made concerning the Great Pyramid of Gizeh, and a number of other sites not so well known. Another meaningful body of material is contained in the "Palestine Readings," given for people who were told they had been together during the life and times of Jesus. This data includes a description of the Essenes and their part in the advent of the Messiah, and is prophetic of the light thrown upon these mysterious people by the discovery of the Dead Sea Scrolls in 1948, fully ten years later.

Many personal readings were given in guiding the vocations and health—spiritual, mental, and physical—of hundreds of persons. Some of this was guidance through his interpretation of other people's dreams. Cayce, himself, had many precognitive dreams.

He, of course, guided his own life and that of his family by his clairvoyance. Finally, he guided the work of the Association with the various committees and study groups organized to carry on its work. Much of this was prophetic. Hardly a move was taken in those days by the Association without the help of the psychic sources.

And yet, prophecy was not the main concern of Edgar Cayce. It was respected and heeded when given, but, just as we in our dreams don't look for predictive messages, so it was with Cayce. Helpfulness was the rule, and prophecy is helpful. Thus was it given. It was both volunteered and sought.

For, of course, he and many others did ask for answers to the riddle of the future. They asked about everything that is humanly possible to ask—about marriage, careers, ending of wars and financial problems. Sometimes they asked about very unusual things, such as oil wells, and buried treasure, about the future of air travel (back when the dirigible was really big!) and they received startling answers at times.

The year 1924 marked a turning point in Edgar's Cayce's life. He gave a reading on Psychic Sources on February 9, just a few weeks before his forty-seventh birthday. It predicted that he would bring through his psychic gifts "joy, peace, and quiet" to the masses and multitudes. This would be done through the efforts, however, of other individuals.

In 1924, the reading went on, after the twentieth of February, when influences astrologically would be those of Pisces (Edgar Cayce's sign) and the sun, he would go forward to develop his psychic and occult abilities for the benefit of great numbers of people that would turn to him.

This reading then foretold that all of his work in this lifetime would be judged by the public according to his own spiritual life, and his manner of living.

He was told to teach psychic and occult ability.

All this unfolded in the latter part of his life.

17

On a clearing among the sand dunes at Fort Story, on Cape Henry, guarding the entrance to the Chesapeake Bay, stands a large, stone cross. Here, every Easter morning, sunrise services are held by devout citizens as the sun slides up out of the ocean and seagulls cry and wheel beyond the gentle surf.

This was the place where in April, 1607, a group of 104 Englishmen rowed ashore to seek their fortunes in the wilderness that then was Virginia. They planted a cross on the shore of Drayton's "Virginia, Earth's only Paradise." They were set on finding gold, the Northwest Passage, and some Indians to convert. They also planned to send home commodities.

They had lost sixteen of their number in the four-month crossing, and after they went to Jamestown, a malarial lowland, they suffered privation and sickness that whittled them down to fifty-three. The history of this nation was indeed begun with a cross.

For three centuries, Cape Henry remained a windswept wilderness of silent sands and forbidding swampland. Toward 1900 there grew up around the Coast Guard station a couple of miles south of the first landing site, a tiny community of perhaps a hundred people, one hotel, one grocery store, and an Episcopal church which was shared by the Methodists.

By 1925, Virginia Beach had grown a little, but it certainly was not a place where you'd invest your money anticipating a real estate boom, nor was it a likely place for even a first-rate clairvoyant to hang out his shingle. And yet, Edgar Cayce was told he should leave Dayton, Ohio, where he had lived for several years, and settle in this lonesome outpost.

The destinies of Edgar Cayce and Virginia Beach seemed to have a mysterious affinity. He was told both in his readings and his dreams that this was the place for him, and that a large institution for learning would be built there, as well as a hospital.

He was told that he should be near large bodies of water

18

for the best use of his powers. In all his incarnations, water had been of great significance for him, and many events important in his development had taken place near water.

Water, so the readings say, is the symbol of life, or spirit, or of the relationship between God and man, or man and his fellowman. Its spiritual symbolism is expressed in our ritual of baptism. So for him, it was particularly significant that his work entered its most important phase after he came to Virginia Beach and settled in the "old headquarters" on Arctic Avenue. This was near a lake separated from the ocean by only a few hundred yards. Here he was to live and give readings for twenty years until his death at 67.

The Cayce Hospital, which came about as predicted within a few years after he settled there, was built on the highest sand dune at Virginia Beach, overlooking the Atlantic, commanding a view of beaches and ocean. Back of it broods the Cape Henry Desert, a symbol of contrast between primeval history and the twentieth century—a reminder of how impenetrable and vast is the mind of man—and how our explorations remain on the edge, only, of its mysteries!

While still in Dayton, Cayce had dreams for several weeks of "a ship off the coast of Virginia where a very hilarious party was going on." People were fishing and making good catches.

When he asked for an interpretation, he was told that it meant that many people would become interested in his new interpretaton of life, as symbolized by the many people on the ship, and their "fishing" (for knowledge) and "catching fish." These symbols, he said, show the "special, specific work that is to be done by individuals . . . the truth of the fact more apparent to all, the work cut out, or set." The individual "fish" caught meant "a lesson to the chosen people that will give the closer understanding between the laws and lessons as were given to a world through the peoples whom the Master came to save."

Another dream earlier that year had told him that "from this place, Virginia Beach, will flow out a great force which will build greater forces or power that will be discovered by means of the phenomena. Not that there will not be hardships, yet let each know, now, when established in the

19

correct place, we will build, knowing we are following the suggestions, the outline from the Force [God] in which we gain the knowledge of all. . . ."

Some others closely associated with Cayce also had dreams predicting the major events of the Cayce work. One person reported for interpretation: "Then I saw a hospital. It was a good one and seemed the result of Henry S's donation. . . ."

The university and the hospital became realities, but only for a few years. They were lost after the 1929 crash, but hopes of their revival have remained with many members of the group. As early as 1931, it was asked if the University could be rehabilitated, and Cayce answered that this was possible.

The hospital building was regained in 1954, when the A.R.E. was able to sell the old headquarters and buy it back. It had changed hands a number of times since 1931, having been a night club, a Navy Nurse's home, and, at the time of its restoration to the A.R.E., it was a Shriners' home. Painted on the walls in the living room were, appropriately, scenes of Egypt with pyramids, palm trees, and burnoosed desert people, reminding everyone of the place Egypt has in the prophecies of old, and its ancient influence on the story of mankind.

How much significance, too, for those to whom the fatherhood of God, the brotherhood of man—the Masonic ideals—mean much! For Cayce had predicted it would be these very ideals upon which would be built the peace of the world!

Those first Englishmen who came to Virginia looking for gold had no idea that it could heal more than economic problems. But, Cayce said, there was gold in the sands that could heal ailing bodies! He told many persons to lie in the warm sands of the resort city and to take "sand packs" for the beneficial effects of the gold there.

"Of all the resorts on the East Coast, Virginia Beach will be the first and the longest lasting of the increasing of the population, valuation, and activities. Hence, we would give, the future is good," said Cayce in 1932. A boom began just after World War II. Now the city ranks third largest in the state. An annual estimate published in the Virginia Beach *Beacon*, November 1, 1967, by the University of Virginia's Bureau of Population and Economic Research, gave the city's population as 145,843. The town has come a long way since the days of its first "gingerbread" hotel, the Princess Anne . . . and one hundred citizens.

Norfolk, also, was in for a good future. "With the years that are to come, conditions that are to arise, as we find, eventually—and this within the next thirty years—Norfolk, with its environs, is to be the chief port on the East Coast, this not excepting Philadelphia or New York; the second being rather in the New England area" (August 27, 1932).

According to "Earth Changes," a booklet written by a geologist who studied the readings, "In 1957 Norfolk Harbor and the Port of Newport News together shipped and imported a total of 59,920 short tons of cargo. Ports of the 'Delaware River and tributaries' were second with 47,569; New York Harbor was third with 42,003; Baltimore Harbor and Channels, Md., handled 32,044; and Portland Harbor, Me., was fifth with 12,935. (U.S. Bureau Census, 1959, table 776.)

"The opening of the Hampton Roads Bridge Tunnel took place in 1957, and in October of this same year approval was granted for construction of the 200-million dollar Chesapeake Bay Bridge Tunnel," the author of "Earth Changes" states further, in reference to a prediction that changes in Norfolk and vicinity would start around 1958. "As the longest fixed-crossing in the world, this structure would make the Norfolk area a "port" for auto and truck traffic along the east coast. In 1959, the engineering and cost analyses for two huge new general cargo facilities at Newport News and Norfolk were completed."

My own recollections of Edgar Cayce are vivid, however confined they are to brief encounters. I remember him with a great deal of understanding that I didn't have then. I had just celebrated my twenty-first birthday, was a newspaper reporter for the Norfolk *Ledger-Dispatch* (now the *Ledger-Star)* and was not about to believe in fortunetellers!

Before 1944 I had never heard of Edgar Cayce and not until June and Harmon Bro came down from Chicago did I find out about him. They were here to learn more about this man of whom Dr. Bro's mother, Margueritte Harmon Bro, had written in the *Coronet* Magazine article, "Miracle Man of Virginia Beach." I met the Bros through my mother, to whom they had been introduced at a Methodist Church function.

Edgar Cayce's birthday was traditionally celebrated each year with a fund-raising party at the old headquarters on Arctic Avenue. On this March 18, my mother and I arrived at the green-shingled headquarters building which was set against a lovely backdrop, Lake Holly. On the way toward the office entrance we passed a doorway where, tall and brooding and alone, stood Edgar Cayce.

A lean, kindly man, he looked down at us from his vantage, a rather thoughtful smile on his face. He did not of course recognize us and so we merely nodded and went on by. But the memory of that strange personage whose reverie we had momentarily broken will never leave me. He stood in a relaxed pose, in his shirtsleeves, hands on hips, gazing out at the world and thinking—what? Perhaps he was tired and welcomed the moment he had taken from the demands of an ever-needful humanity. Perhaps he read our minds, or at least our auras, as I later learned he could do. Perhaps he saw the vast doubt we shared about him. We were not sure just why we had attended this particular party, but were drawn by the Bros' earnest persuasion that we know more about this man.

Later that summer I attended a reading session. Well, I didn't really attend it. I was such an unbeliever then that they were afraid my negative attitude would be a disturbing influence on the sleeping seer! So while Harmon was inside recording the proceedings in the little corner office (Cayce's son Hugh Lynn, normally in charge, was in the army over in Europe), June and I sat outside on the grass, leaning against a tree, trying to catch what was going on through the open windows.

We could understand very little . . . we heard only the rise and fall of Edgar Cayce's voice as he spoke in his self-imposed sleep. It was maddening. I really was getting curious, in spite of my prejudices, and wished very much that I was inside.

"Why don't you ask for a reading?" June urged me many

times. Harmon was quite enthusiastic by now, after spending several months with the Cayces, and was increasingly respectful of Cayce's ability. He and June had readings, but I remained uncertain.

Edgar Cayce was to die within months. I never had my reading. Later, however, I did begin to study the readings and parallel material in the A.R.E. library. I became a member of the Virginia Beach Study Group, met and talked with many of his friends, and grew aware of the undercurrents of feelings about him on the part of local townspeople. To this day the feelings appear to be mixed. To those who knew him, he was a great soul. To many who had readings from him, and were associated with him through the physical readings and their effects on the health of local people, he was "Dr. Cayce." Interesting testimonies are recorded in the files from Virginia Beach people who saw the results of his readings on their lives. Yet many others have never known, or cared to know, about the work. Over the years, at times, I have heard doubting remarks about the beliefs among Association members, particularly their belief in reincarnation. But in knowing the people in the Association, and in studying the data myself, I have gained a better insight into life.

For a long time I could not accept the idea of reincarnation, which is part and parcel of the Cayce phenomenon. But as I attended lectures by Hugh Lynn Cayce, Harmon Bro, Eula Allen, Esther Wynne, Hannah and Noah Miller, Harold Reilly, Lydia J. Schrader Gray, and many others, my sympathy for the work grew and so did my understanding.

I regret never having really talked to Edgar Cayce or obtaining a reading. But I have one memory I value—the memory of a man standing in a doorway, casting his glances at sky and budding trees of spring, and thinking his own thoughts about a world that is so ready to see the worst and so slow to accept the best.

* * *

The people who knew Cayce first hand, who worked and grew with his work, have lived to see many of his predictions come to pass. They have also seen new people come to help, people who never had a reading but who were attracted by the story told in books, newspaper accounts, magazine articles. Cayce had predicted that those who weren't ready for the "work" would not be with it long. Those who have stayed through the years have had a long time to observe the many ways in which human nature reacts to the unknown, and have been witnesses to a unique kind of experience in history involving God's ways with His children.

There seems to be a testing that takes place. But the human will being what it is, and the human capacity to change and drift, react, and blossom with almost no discernible pattern, many come back who first were repelled. A few drop away, finding other interests or simply becoming discouraged. The work has its requirements: one must seek to be a channel of service to others, put away prejudices and materialistic tendencies, and come with an open mind.

Without these basic qualities, those who have lived through the testing period agree, one could never make it.

Cayce said in his "Work Readings" that the A.R.E. should be first a research organization, then an enlightening one. The research should precede the enlightenment. It would be "in keeping with those things that are sacred, those that are true, those that are helpful, and yet being tolerant to all. . . ."

Furthermore, its members are to present to others only those experiences that have proven valid at first hand. Those who didn't find within themselves that an idea was good shouldn't advocate it.

He said that those who had found this work compatible should never find fault with others who disagree with them, but that they should "glory in the promises of thy Lord, thy Master, thy brother, in those things that He would do in the earth through thine feeble efforts."

There is throughout the readings a pervasive compassion for those who committed themselves to the task of first living, and then presenting the standpoints in the Cayce files. Whether it was experimenting with the effects of atomidine and prayer on one's dreams, or whether it was taking osteopathic treatments, or whether it was speaking kindly to one who was unkind, the *research* in life should come first, before one talked about it.

24

Study groups sprang up, following the Norfolk Study Group One, which Edgar Cayce led. Now there are over two hundred such groups all over the country, and more forming all the time. These attempt to guide the research and enlightenment at the "grass roots," so to speak. They are formed to study and to try Cayce's numerous suggestions to a better life. Some of these follow the "Search for God" Books One and Two, written by members of the first A.R.E. Study Group during months of efforts to apply the wisdom of the readings. This group had literally prayed, suffered, and wept its way through the readings, giving guidance and counsel in order to bring to others what they had found.

Never do the Cayce students proselyte, nor insist that anyone take part. The facts are there at 67th Street, Virginia Beach, Virginia. How important they are remains always for the individual to find out for himself. They can seem inconsequential, even ridiculous and to some they have. Or they can mean the difference between life and death, and they have, to uncounted numbers.

In the following pages we will present the major prophecies of Edgar Cayce, taking "first things first" as he emphasized. The readings on World Affairs, given in the twenties through the early forties in answer to questions about global problems, present the case of his veracity for themselves, as do the many on scientific developments of recent years, which Cayce predicted forty years ago. This book comes to be written with what seems to be excellent timing: the great upheavals that allegedly will affect millions of people were predicted to begin in 1968 and continue to 1998. An atmosphere of revelation new seems to be present as we see history unfold in the light of the Cayce predictions. To have lived with the readings as the predicted events were ticked off through the decades has been for the Cayce students a unique manifestation of clairvoyance. But one becomes used to it. As each important world event takes place, one is no longer surprised.

As for Edgar Cayce, he seemed to step aside and join the onlookers with their peculiar brand of savoir faire regarding their inside position to Time's secrets. In his simple wisdom, he regarded it all with a great deal of patience for those who scoffed. He of course did not live to see many of his world prophecies come true, because they were about events following his death. Others are happening now, and some are still to be proven.

In his readings he equated the Spirit of God with Time, Space, and the useful virtue Patience. He explained prophecy against that equation. However, it is one thing to repeat the formula, and another to get up before the class and explain it. Given a little of each—Time, Space, and Patience—I will attempt to present some of what Cayce said about prophecy.

II

THE NEW AGE

Hell, her numbers full,
Thenceforth shall be for ever shut. Meanwhile,
The world shall burn, and from her ashes spring
New heaven and earth, wherein the just shall dwell,
And, after all their tribulations long,
See golden days, fruitful of golden deeds,
With joy and love triumphing, and fair truth.

Milton's *Paradise Lost*, Book Three,
300-335

This is the New Age?

Low morals, spreading anarchy, juvenile crime, drug addiction and a war which half the nation condemns; riots that bring death and injury to hundreds, dissent that divides us: This is the New Age?

"What do you think will happen in the twenty-first century?" a scientist was asked recently.

"I'm not convinced we'll have a twenty-first century," was the answer.

In trying to reconcile the Cayce predictions for an ever-better world during the last part of this century, we are hard put to figure out the inconsistencies of what we see and what the readings say is happening.

But, despite wars, riots, dire predictions of earth upheavals, we are reminded that this is a time of change, and like the bull in the china shop, it's upsetting a lot of dishes.

It is, in the words of St. Paul, "the day of the Lord," and a lot of housecleaning is being done, according to the Cayce data. In passages that are awe-inspiring in their majesty, we are told: "That as has been promised through the prophets and the sages of old—the time and half time—has been and is being fulfilled in this day and generation; and that seen there will again appear in the earth—that one through whom many will be called to meet those who are preparing the way for His day in the earth. The Lord then will come, even as ye have seen Him go . . . when those who are His have made the way clear and passable for Him to come."

"The way clear and passable" seems to refer to spiritual conditions in the earth. We are suddenly aware of the magnitude of the many basic reforms now being wrought within the Church, which are in keeping with our new understanding of righteousness in this day. We are sharply aware of the great struggle between two nations which is primarily of a spiritual nature, for America, founded upon religious principles, is at natural odds with a nation which denies the very existence of God.

Then, as such reforms and struggles take place in the ideological arenas of this age and the way is there being made "passable," we see again that it is by the will of man—of man making his will one with God's—that he makes for himself a better world in which the Christ can abide.

Man seems ready for a step up in his evolution, according to the Cayce readings. We are poised on the beginning of the Aquarian Age, following the one just ended—the Piscean—which has lasted for two thousand years under the symbol of the "fish" of the early Christian Church. These ages overlap and we will not begin to fully understand all that the present one brings until the turn of the century. By then, we will see the Day of the Lord at a more completed stage, not only in our imaginations, but in actuality. It will be the beginning of the Millenium. "As given," says the reading, "for a thousand years He will walk and talk with men of every clime. Then, in groups, in masses, and then they shall reign of the first resurrection for a thousand years, for this will be when the changes materially come."

It appears that first He, the Christ, will be in the hearts of mankind then and will begin to walk and talk with men in our physical world. Meanwhile, we will experience the effect of the Christ upon the hearts of individuals.

28

It will be in the hearts of leaders, as has been in the past, as the following example shows:

"In the manner as He sat at the peace conference in Geneva, in the heart and soul of a man not reckoned by many as an even unusually godly man [Woodrow Wilson] yet raised for a purpose, and he chose rather to be a channel of His thought for the world. So as there has been, so will it be, until the time as set. As was given of Him, not given to man to know the time or the period of the end, nor to man, save by their constituting themselves a channel through which He may speak."

The year 1998 is given in a number of readings for the time of this great event. By that time, the world will have seen much drastic change and upheaval of both a geologic and social nature. Thus far the change has been gradual, but will become more pronounced.

"In 1998 we may find a great deal of the activities as have been wrought by the gradual changes that are coming about," states another reading. "These are at the periods when the cycle of the solar activity, or the years are related to the sun's passage through the various spheres of activity, become paramount, or tantamount to the change between the Piscean and the Aquarian Age. This is a gradual, not a cataclysmic, activity in the experience of the earth in this period."

What specifically can we expect for 1998? The readings firmly state that there will be "less of wars" even before then, that peace will come to the world, and that man will learn more and more how to benefit from scientific discoveries still in the offing!

For centuries people have been predicting the end of the world and have been fooled every time. Even the Christians of the early church expected it in their day. People have been preparing for it in every generation since. Why should we believe it's really happening now?

The answer is: Look within. If you have ever experienced a moment of true brotherly concern for another person, or expressed a kindness to someone, or showed patience toward an erring child, you know something of the New Age and what it will bring. It has been gathering force throughout the ages in just this way. It will happen because the way has been made "clear and passable" not only by formal action taken in self-reform in the church, but by the good we ourselves are responsible for.

In this reading on "Spiritual Evolution" given September 22, 1939, a student asked, "What will the Aquarian Age mean to mankind as regards physical, and mental and spiritual development?"

Cayce replied tartly: "Think ye this might be answered in a word? These are as growths. What meant that awareness as just indicated? In the Piscean Age, in the center of same, we had the entrance of Emmanuel or God among men, see? What did that mean? The same will be meant by the full consciousness of the ability to communicate with or to be aware of the relationships to the Creative Forces, God, and the uses of same in material environs.

"Then, as to what will these be—only those who accept same will even become aware of what's going on about them!

"How few realize the vibratory forces as create influences from one individual to another, when they are even in the same vibratory force or influence! And yet, ye ask what will the Aquarian Age bring in mind, in body, in experience!"

As the entrance of Emmanuel or God among men meant the salvation of mankind in the Piscean Age, so will the next great step be given man: the full consciousness that he can communicate with God! How many of us even comprehend the advent of God two thousand years ago? The New Age we are entering will hold for us just as tremendous a concept in our evolution!

In 1942 a young man asked, "When this [peace] does come about, can you advise some of the world conditions and how to meet them?"

The answer was, "This will depend upon much of the activities of those who have the establishing of the relationships.

"Individually, know that right, justice, mercy, patience —as was represented and presented by Him—the Prince of Peace—is the basis upon which the new world order *must* eventually be established before there *is* peace.

"Then, innately, mentally, and manifestedly in self, pre-

30

pare self for cooperative measures in all phases of human relations in this direction."

Another man, concerned about his personal responsibility in helping to bring about world peace, asked in March, 1944: "What can I do to help bring about the New Age?"

He was told, "As just indicated, you will have to practice it in your own life. These are the manners and channels through which this might be better expressed by this particular entity."

Does the New Age, then, depend upon God's will or man's? If this man was told that he could help bring it about by "practicing" it in his own life, what good was the age-old prophecy anyway? What if this man decided *not* to practice the new understanding of peace and brotherhood (which is ever new, it seems, in every age)? If he said, "I will not," would the New Age grind to a halt?

Well, it seems that the New Age is coming about both because of—and in spite of—mankind! God doesn't really need man. Man needs God. But man can, by his own free will, *delay* or *hasten* fulfillment of God's plan.

This is indicated plainly in the following message to a group seeking spiritual help: "And so may ye, as seekers for divine guidance, be uplifted and thus may ye hasten the day when war will be no more."

During the dark days of World War II, many such messages were given to persons bowed down by the sorrows of the time. A week before Pearl Harbor, (November 29, 1941) this heartening word was given for Study Group One: "Though troubled and a blood-stained world, thy prayer, thy blessing may bring a new hope, and may blossom into joy on earth, peace among men."

Invariably, when people or groups asked for help in what to do about bringing lasting peace, the responsibility was thrown right back into their own laps. The search for world peace became just such another personal challenge to a woman of sixty-three who asked, "Will I live to see this war ended and peace and happiness in America?"

"The peace and happiness must first be within self," she was told. "You will be living when war is ended, but when peace is established—that's something else!"

31

Eight years later, she wrote "My life reading gave me a clearer idea of my responsibility and obligation to serve humanity. . . ." She reported that in spite of bad health, nervous exhaustion, and a crippling fall which left her in a wheelchair, at seventy-one she became a diagnostician and found a measure of the peace and happiness she had sought within herself. For her the New Age had already come!

The motto on the Great Seal of the United States, *Novus Ordo Seclorum,*" means "A new order of ages." It is not by chance that America has that mystical motto, according to what the Cayce readings say about this nation's role in the world's destiny.

America's Role in the New Age

"The spirituality of the American people will be rather as the criterion of that as is to become the world's forces, for, as has been given in that of the peace table, there sat the Master in the American people; with the brotherhood of the world accepted, war was at an end. Without [the brotherhood of the world] there will again come the Armageddon, and in same there will be seen that the Christian forces will again move westward!"

So spoke Cayce on October 9, 1926, during a period of great scandal and immorality on the part of America, reveling in unmatched national prosperity and pursuing at the same time a policy of isolationism from the rest of the world. This was the "Roaring 20's."

It was this nation, Cayce reminds us, which was founded by devout and religious men, and which declares on its money, "In God We Trust." Specifically, as was mentioned earlier, Cayce pointed to President Wilson, who, although not known to be particularly godly, was yet "raised for a purpose" and who "chose to be a channel of His thought for the world" as he strove to create peaceful measures in Geneva. This is elaborated upon in another reading given January 15, 1932:

"Some years ago (this, we understand, is out of line with what many would have one believe) there was a Peace Table, and about same were gathered representatives of every nation under the sun! In the soul of the represenlative of the United States sat the Prince of Peace—yet many would have you believe, that in the economical world, the financial world, had that man never left his home, his own shores, the world would be better today. Not so; for 'Ye shall pay every whit'; for 'The heavens and earth may pass away, but My Word shall not' are the words of Him who made the world.

"As to whether it will be in three years or five years [that peace comes] depends upon those who would rally to 'I will make of my life a channel of blessing to *someone* today.' "

In a biography published in 1960, President Wilson was championed by his physician and naval aide, Rear Admiral Cary T. Grayson, who served during Wilson's two White House terms. Admiral Grayson asserted that Wilson would have given his very life if he could have saved the League of Nations. In a conversation on March 25, 1920, Wilson told Grayson that he would run for a third term "even if I thought it would cost me my life." He died February 3, 1924, only three years following his presidency, from the effects of a stroke brought about by his strenuous crusade for the League.

All during the years before World War II, individuals asked if America would be drawn into war and what could be done. "What is the outlook for war?" was asked in the thirties.

"If America acts as it prays" she would not be drawn into the war, Cayce repeated.

But three months before Pearl Harbor, this hope was withdrawn. On August 31, 1941, the picture changed. No longer did Cayce state that we might be spared involvement, but that war was imminent for us.

It was man's will which had made the difference. A study of one nation's going to war affords us an opportunity to learn how individuals, like nations, create their own destiny: prophecy is only flexible to a certain point of no return. God will not always wait for us to turn to Him, but permits His laws to operate. If a man or a country continues to act in a way that leads to disaster, the disaster will come.

The reading of August 31, 1941, that marked the turning point in America's destiny stated: "It is evident that there are strenuous conditions imminent in the affairs of the land, owing to thought as respecting the relationships in varied portions of the world.

"And, as has been and is indicated, unusual combinations are being made; and those individual groups or nations that have heretofore manifested friendly or brotherly relationships are now seen to be as enemies . . ."

Thus he predicted the reversal in Japan's attitude toward the United States from that of friendship to enmity.

Following the prophecy of war for America, this same reading predicted the date war would end and discussed the principles upon which world peace would be built: those inherent in American ideals, including the brotherhood of man, and of Masonry!

"For with those changes that will be wrought, Americanism—the ism—with the universal thought that is expressed and manifested in the brotherhood of man into group thought, as expressed by the Masonic Order—will be the eventual rule in the settlement of affairs in the world.

"Not that the world is to become a Masonic Order, but the principles that are embraced in same will be the basis upon which the new order of peace is to be established in '44 and '45."

This reading also advised Americans to guard against Communism and Fascism, and to take a stand for Christ and His principles rather than becoming involved with questionable groups. "A great number of individuals formulated into groups who have declared specific or definite policies will be questioned as to purpose and as to the ideal. Some of such will be drawn into coalition with questionable groups."

There was once a time when nations lived unto themselves. Even America practiced isolationism, and considering her role in the affairs of the world, it is surprising that she should have refused to join the League of Nations. According to Cayce, it was Americans who must carry the spirit of cooperation with them to other lands, in the postwar world of twenty years ago.

It was December 8, 1941, the day after Pearl Harbor, when this message was dropped in the lap of one person seeking information: "While there will not be the reversal of the capitalistic system, there is to be the establishment more and more of the cooperative basis—in local, state, county, national, and international activities. Cooperation must form the basis of activities, such as has been indicated here, and is to be applied not only in the home, but in corporations, in mines, in manufacturing, in the nations—more and more.

"There will be the greater abilities, the greater possibilities—not of America becoming again as the land to which others will flee, but *Americans* must go to the other lands and carry cooperation with them!"

We think of the Marshal Plan, the Peace Corps, and of the many cooperative measures we have taken in helping the less fortunate nations during those years. International cooperation has been created through many agencies, including the North Atlantic Treaty Organization, Organization of American States, and other regional groups.

It was a war-sick world by May, 1944. On May 10, someone asked Cayce, "What can be done specifically by the American people to bring about a speedy, lasting peace?"

Consistently, Cayce continued to put the responsibility with ourselves. "We haven't the American people," he said. "The thing is to start with yourself. Unless you can bring about within yourself that which you would have in the nation or in any particular land, don't offer it to others."

On May 14, another person asked for affirmations or little prayers that might be used in praying for peace. "As to affirmations: these should be towards that of peace through the next six to eight months. For then through this period will the earth and its peoples be passing through the most strenuous period of the world's history since the Master walked in the earth!"

The six to eight months following May, 1944, held the heaviest destruction by American and British bombing raids on Nazi-held Europe of the entire war. Two-thirds of the destruction was carried on *after* July, 1944! The year 1944 saw the great invasion of Europe by the Allies in June; the breakthrough at St. Lo; the Battle of the Bulge.

The Japanese stepped up their attack on China late in 1944 and the war in the Pacific was being fought with the heaviest losses and fighting in which Saipan, Guam, the Philippines fell to the Allies by Christmas.

After January, 1945, the worst was ever. The predicted eight months of trial, the worst in history since the time of the Master two thousand years ago, had come to pass.

Leaders in the New Age

In 1942, a young woman of twenty-five was told, "Be *glad* you have the opportunity to be alive at this time, and to be a part of that preparation for the coming influences of a spiritual nature that must rule the world. These are indicated and these are part of thy experience. Be happy of it, and give thanks daily for it."

The "Day of the Lord," that St. Paul foretold, is coming, according to Cayce. "The Lord will come . . . when those who are his have made the way clear" for His return.

Who are "those who are His?"

Evidently, they are among us now, seemingly quite ordinary people—because they are people we know. They are leaders who are quietly carrying out their task, we gather. Throughout the files are mentioned appearances of many who will prepare the way. They are coming to leadership at a time when they are sorely needed—a high-minded breed of individuals who have incarnated in large numbers in recent years.

Among these are several outstanding world spiritual leaders who were incarnated around 1935 and 1936. According to one reference, St. Martin, patron saint of France, is to serve in some manner in 1989 at the age of fifty-four.

As early as 1931, a woman was told that she would see the "greatest development in spiritual affairs that the world has known."

There seems to be an intensified incarnation of Atlanteans now, or those souls who had incarnations in the Atlantean civilization. (See chapter on Atlantis.) Especially was there an influx of these souls between the years 1909 and 1913 inclusive. Now fifty-five to fifty-seven years old, these are doubtless among those in authority in positions everywhere today throughout the world.

These people may "rule or ruin" the character of man's condition, bringing from Atlantis their extremes in character—the very worst, the very best. They have strong emotional and mental traits combined with a past record of "engorgement of carnal influences in the experience of others, of self-indulgence." They also were scientifically advanced, and so possess technical knowledge, or an inherent ability in technology.

On July 4, 1939, a thirty-one-year-old music teacher, Protestant, with unorthodox leanings, was told that she was "one of those of the new order of the Atlanteans that will either make for a great development" or help repeat the errors of the past. These errors are described as "of the natural tendencies of the material aspect of the world" at the time of Atlantis when that nation had become proud and self-destructive.

Others were similarly told that they were among "those individuals upon whom the real future of the state or nation will depend" and "may in this experience be the mother of those who may fill high places; . . . be well guarded in the law of the Lord, for it is perfect and will convert the souls of men."

A sixteen-year-old boy asked on June 24, 1940: " Will I or any of my immediate family reincarnate with Mr. Cayce in 1998?"

He was told: "This is not to be given, or things of such natures, but is to be determined by the desire, the need, the application of those who may desire to do so."

Another excerpt stated: "For as has been indicated now, in the next few years, there will be many entrances of those who are to prepare the way for the new race, the experiences of man, that may be a part of those activities in preparation for the Day of the Lord."

To another: "All that are in the earth today are thy brothers. Those that have gradually forgotten God entirely have been eliminated, and there has come—now—and will come at the close of this next year [1943] the period when there will be no part of the globe where man has not had the opportunity to hear 'The Lord He is God.'

"And, as has been indicated, when this period has been accomplished, then the New Era, the New Age is to begin. Will ye have a part of it, or will ye let it pass by and be merely a hanger-on, or one upon whom your brother—the Lord, thy Christ—may depend?"

III

CHOOSE THOU!

"There is this day set before thee good and evil. Choose thou!"

Jane Harrington looked across the breakfast table at Claude, her young husband. "I dreamed," she said slowly, "of a weak-minded boy." She frowned. "What could it mean?"

Claude swallowed a sudden sense of foreboding with a gulp of coffee and replied, "It's probably a symbol of something the matter with your head." He returned her troubled glance with what he hoped was a grin.

"I am *not* weak-minded!" Jane pretended insult, tossing her lovely bobbed hair. It was 1925, she had been married one month, and she resented the dream's intrusion on her happiness.

"Was that all you remember?" Claude asked lightly.

"That's all. Could it be precognitive?"

"Oh, it doesn't have to be literally so. . . . It can be symbolic, you know, of some conditions you might be running into."

Jane was silent for a moment as she stared out of the window at the city skyline, as if the answer skipped along the tops of the buildings there in the blue summer sky. "Or could it actually be the prediction that . . . someone we know . . . is going to have a . . . retarded child?"

Now Claude fell silent. Finally he said, "It could be."

The Harringtons were no ordinary dreamers. For several years before his marriage, Claude had been a student of dreams. He had been recording his dreams and sending them to Edgar Cayce in Virginia Beach for interpretation. His bride, a bright psychology major planning to work for her master's degree, became fascinated with the project and began recording her own dreams for the southern psychic.

This particular dream was so disturbing to Claude that he decided to write Cayce that very day. "I am indeed anxious to get an interpretation of Jane's dream of a weak-minded boy or child," he wrote, "for we have had certain discussions and maybe it is a warning to her. Of course I am guessing."

They had already learned much of the nature of dreams, from past discourses given them by Cayce. They knew that dreams often are symbolic, rather than literal. Thus a dream of death usually means the "death" of one's past and the beginning of a new and better future; "putting on clothes" symbolizes for most people the putting on of various states of mind or attitudes.

However, Cayce's reading shortly after was not reassuring. He told them that "any condition becoming reality is first dreamed." It was, he said, "a projection of thought, of conditions" that were indeed possible in the future.

When Jane became pregnant a year later, they set aside all doubts. This would be a very special child, for the Harringtons had faith that through preparation and dedication of themselves to high ideals founded in their religion they could produce a great spiritual leader.

Dreams, they argued, did not have to come true—not that kind. And their confidence was later bolstered by further information from Cayce that although there were laws in operation which governed the possibility of dreams being an accurate indicator of the future, the "maybe" factor was always very strong.

Unfortunately, their joy in anticipating their child was marred. Quarrels and misunderstandings arose, and the conflict was not to be resolved. Even as they looked forward to the birth of their child, they were torn by their growing estrangement.

On April 4, 1927, a son was born to them. He was normal. Now, there were to be many readings for this new little person in whom the unhappy parents still placed such high hopes.

After the excitement of the new arrival had worn off, the Harringtons turned away from each other with mounting bitterness. Then came the stock market crash . . . a time when fears for the future ran high and lives were drastically changed overnight. Within a few years, the Harringtons found themselves in the divorce courts. Jane was given full custody of young Edward, who was never to see his father afterward. Edward later wistfully wrote to Edgar Cayce that he had tried to get in touch with his father, to no avail.

Edward possessed a brilliant mind. He studied in a university for several years and valiantly followed his leanings to spiritual matters. He had a high temper, of which Cayce had warned. At twenty-five he had a mental breakdown and was admitted to an asylum. Thus, his mother's precognition two years before he was born had become a tragic reality.

Jane, and all those involved, may well have asked years later, as she did when she first "saw" the event: "What could it mean?"

In this sad account of the fulfillment of a twenty-seven-year-old prophetic dream, we have a study in precognition and the many questions it raises. It is more than just an emotional experience, a mysterious experience; it has lessons not only for the people it involved, but also for anyone who cares to seek them out.

Our first reaction to such a story is perhaps best expressed with a shudder. Who, we cry, needs such previews of tragedy? And yet, we want to *know*, transfixed as we are midway between dread and anticipation, whatever the future may hold!

The reason for this lies in what the Cayce readings tell us is our "birthright." For in our dreams, he stated, we are given our own personal prophecies. In addition, these visions from the subconscious and superconscious warn, prepare, advise, rebuke, goad, remind, inspire, cheer, reassure, chide, and guide the dreamer toward doing better. If we don't remember our dreams, or are poor interpreters of them, we miss out on our birthright. By recording them daily, we can increase our memory and ability to interpret the messages that are meant for our use.

As for Jane and Claude, what went wrong? We have, thanks to their intelligent and avid interest in dreams, a fund of information on the subject which has contributed greatly to our knowledge. At the same time, no amount of knowledge prevented them from ultimate grief and disaster. Claude had dreams to indicate that their child would become the spiritual light they had hoped for, and they were apparently encouraged to believe this by Cayce's analysis. But there were the *two* possibilities which awaited them: what could have tipped the scales against the happier ending?

According to the readings, the answer, painful as it is, lies in the failure of the parents to live up to their sacred marriage vows, to give the boy the stability he needed in order to carry out his life work. He was brilliant but highstrung—his very sanity depending upon the kind of home life created around him. Had he been more stable, he perhaps would not have been affected by these conditions.

We would not judge this beautiful and highly motivated couple of the "roaring 20's" and their hope of rearing together a spiritual leader. We only know that Edgar Cayce gave us, and them, in their earnest soul-searching during those early days of their marriage, the understanding that "we find there are no coincidences, or chance coincidences. Each and every individual follows out that line of development of the entity in the present earth plane as it has received from the preceding conditions, and each grain of thought or condition is a consequence of other conditions created by self. And in this particular condition, we find this is a condition wherein the body [Claude] may choose that which will give development for self. For this body should remember this injunction, as was given:

"It is not that one should ascend into the heavens to bring the Force [God] to man, or that one should ascend into the elements, or go into the depths, to bring up the Forces, for there has been set before you, this day, good and evil. Choose that which will bring the better development of self, and in lending to the Lord is the service that man renders to his Maker. . . ."

To another person at another time, Cayce said, "In the spiritual aspects [of life] everything is good. As the individual works out his destiny by application of mind, his experiences become bad or good, depending upon his choices."

See Deuteronomy 30:12-20!

In April, 1930, the Cayce Hospital was admitting patients for treatment according to the suggestions in the readings. Fred Pelham, then fifty and suffering from neurosis of five years' standing, entered on the twenty-second and had his first reading.

He asked the sleeping Cayce, "Is the case curable? If so, approximately how long?"

Cayce answered, "Curable, sure—it's curable! How long? How hard will the body not try, but just get well?"

Evidently, it was a matter of Fred's choice!

His readings called for changes in diet, for sandpacks and violet-ray applications. Later, Fred lay on the beach that stretched below the hospital, covered by the warm sand which he had been told contained gold which was healing to the body.

"Just what can this do for me," he grumbled, "a man who's gone through the crash, lost everything—for a man whose wife has turned against him!" He stared moodily at the blue sky above. The cool salt breezes on his face felt chilly to him. He sighed with the heaviness of Job.

A sense of failure had dogged him here. In his heart he told himself that it had all been too much for one man. His marriage was gone, and he might as well face up to it. Slowly he got up from the sand and brushed it off his body. He thought, "This is crazy. How can lying out here . . . taking those light treatments . . . eating that silly rabbit food change things back home? Crazy doctors, crazy me for thinking they know!"

But he found himself in the water, and the salt sting of it dashed his dark thoughts momentarily away. They washed off with the sand and when he plodded back to the hospital a little later, he discovered he was hungry. "Wonder what they'll have for supper?" he mused. "Rabbit food, no doubt!"

And so the summer went. Fred took his treatments among the other patients and gradually he seemed to be feeling better. He had another reading on August 29, four months after entering. It stated: "When the body physical, body mental, has so attuned itself as to be able to face self and self's obligations, self's relations one with another, in that period there will come changes in the business asso-

43

ciations and business relations such as to enable the body to make that as is builded in the interim in the mental and physical body. . . .

"Three to five weeks . . . and then the body will find that there will be those aids for seemingly unseen sources as will make for the better relations, the better associations, in the marital and domestic relations, and an understanding reached. Do not falter in self."

Fred asked in this reading, "How can the body go about to create the harmony that is desired in the home life?"

The anwer was, "By taking a stand for that as is known in self as to be the proper, the correct relationships as must and will exist, and keep to that as is known, and felt, irrespective of anything else."

By now, Fred had been exposed to the attitude toward prayer and its healing power prevalent at the hospital and engendered by the devout Edgar Cayce himself. The atmosphere of cheerfulness and good will that was breathed in along with the salt air had worked wonders for Fred. His next question was tendered with great sincerity: "What prayer can be held by the body as a guide to that he wishes to attain?"

"May the meditations of my heart, my mind, my body be wholly acceptable in thy sight, My Lord and My Redeemer," was the reply.

His next question was one which he had been pondering for some weeks now, for he had begun to think it might be possible to make a new start at home. He was advised to take things easy in this direction, until he had become strong enough to maintain his equilibrium. "This should not be considered too fast, for the inclination will be to worry over same. Will that as has just been given be held, the place, the position, will be seeking the man as much as the man seeking the place . . ."

On September 20, Fred Pelham was dismissed to return home and to a new life. For him, Edgar Cayce had been the best sort of prophet—and doctor! For Fred was a changed man, and a changed man can do anything—including winning back a place in business, and the woman he loves!

"For remember, the Creative Force [God] has made man with a will of his own. As to what a man will do with same, only he himself *can* know! Only the tendencies and the inclinations may be given; and these, as indicated here, at times have seemed bad choices, and at times there have been helpful influences. These must depend upon the entity himself."

To others, Edgar Cayce expressed much the same thought. He explained to one this: "As He has given, God has fixed the doors . . . . He has fixed the purposes through which man's own activity may pass. Yet He leaves the choice to man."

The attitude of expectancy is very important in directing our future lives. "He that expects—and acts in an expectant manner—consistent with the mental and physical activities—will be rewarded."

And yet, when Cayce gave a prediction, it was often unqualified and seemingly irrevocable. He had predicted that Claude Harrington woud marry Jane months before Claude proposed or was sure he would! A friend of the Harrington's wrote: "You are a wizard when it comes to marrying people. I don't know whether Claude sold the proposition to you or you sold it to him, but he certainly is going to marry the girl in —— and you said it would be in the Southwest and you also said within a year."

Evidently, then, understanding destiny is not as simple as we would hope. "The race is not to the swift, nor the battle to the strong, neither yet bread to the wise, nor yet riches to men of understanding, nor yet favour to men of skill; but time and chance happeneth to them all." (Ecclesiastes 9:11)

What is it that brings order out of chaos, then? To some who asked Edgar Cayce if it were possible to understand, he replied, "His ways are not past finding out, to those who attune themselves to that inner consciousness which is the birthright of each entity—that privilege, that opportunity *given* to each soul. . . ." Thus, man is right in pursuing his attempt to understand destiny a little better, to find his place amidst its mysterious workings.

IV

DESTINY AND THE LAW

"My son, in all thine getting, get understanding" is the biblical injunction.

Cayce added, ". . . and the ability to apply it."

We are living under what he referred to as "Universal Laws" which were in effect for the Harringtons, and have not reportedly gone out of existence since their time.

He said that the purpose of life is "to gain the understanding of all universal laws." The knowledge attained by living these and making them a part of our second nature brings development: spiritual, mental, and even physical.

The application of the law leads to the understanding of the basis upon which destiny is founded. For it is man's use or abuse of the law which is destiny's prime mover.

Man has, furthermore, the gift of free will. If he chooses to break the laws, he must abide by the consequences, for "God is not mocked and whatsoever a man soweth, that must he reap."

It is this Law—the whole gamut of many laws—which undergirds the earth and the universe, unchanging and sure. It is what brings order out of chaos. In a time when there is a breakdown of respect for the laws of both God and man, a look at Edgar Cayce's explanation of the present dilemma of man in the earth seems to be helpful.

It was "lawless men," said Peter, who crucified Jesus of Nazareth. Edgar Cayce was no less concerned with upholding law and order. He inspired respect for one's country, one's leaders, and for the rights of his neighbors. He told us to do all things in "decency and order, doing first things first." He followed Christ's admonition to "render unto Caesar what is Caesar's." Man as he is today must still have laws based on those of God, and once established, the laws must be respected and obeyed.

The current rejection of law and order in favor of anarchy and "mob rule" which Cayce predicted for this age, expressed in race riots, pot parties, student demonstrations, and all the rest, is not in the spirit of the Cayce philosophy. Nor is childish rebellion against one's parents the mature way to change one's world, as the psychologists and Cayce agree. Change comes about by working to improve one's self, coordinating the emotions with the mind, and keeping what is good from the past. This is best expressed by observing the orderly function of the laws of the universe, which direct the movement of planets and temper for us the heat of the sun, as they govern the fate of the humblest child.

In comparing Paul's letter to the law-conscious Romans with what the Cayce readings say, we find a freer interpretation of what law is. It covers every avenue of life, and is to be found, it would seem, as much among the unwritten truths we live by, as those that are in the books. It is to these unwritten laws that Paul seems to be referring, and these are brothers to those in the Cayce files. Nearly all the first ten chapters of the book of Romans speak of these spiritual laws. "I find then a law, that, when I would do good, evil is present with me" (7:21). Paul further speaks of the "law of the Spirit of life in Christ Jesus," the "law of faith," the "law of righteousness" and the "law of works."

The Law of Karma

One of Cayce's most repeated references is to "that first rule, a law that is eternal: The seed sown must one day be reaped." This is a key to understanding reincarnation and karma, which demonstrate the law of cause and effect. It applies not only to the present life we are living, but to past and future lives. Our present life is the result of those we have lived; it is the cause of our future experiences, for they will be determined by our thoughts and actions now. Cayce emphasized the biblical statement: "The Law of the Lord is perfect; it converteth the soul."

We may avoid learning these statutes, much less put them into practice. But they are there and we daily come under the "law." "If you would have friends, be friendly. If you would be loved, be loving." Reminded the sleeping seer: "There are laws—law is love, love is law. . . ."

In the case of the Harringtons, we see that the destiny of their child born into tragic circumstances was ordered for him by his karma. For, if nothing is by chance, and if we create our future, then birth into this or that situation must have its cause. He had been born into this by his actions in a past life, as we interpret it, and was to learn a lesson which his soul would never forget. He was paying for some transgression of spiritual law he had committed long ago. A hard punishment? Yes, but no doubt it was one he had earned; it was therefore appropriate.

And yet his parents, with their free wills in this life, shared the responsibility. How do we decipher this facet of their joint destiny?

Parents attract the children that come to them by their prayers and hopes, as did the Harringtons, or their *lack* of these, as the case may be. They set the stage, so to speak, by the way they live, long before the child is born. This illustrates still another law, the law of attraction. The boy which Claude and Jane received was bright and sensitive, like themselves, but their disharmony was reflected in his very personality through the years in the form of insanity. He was very much their child, their spiritual and mental progeny!

We carry over character traits and influences from past lives. These, therefore, are to be considered in predicting what we will do in this life. This point is made clear in the case of a young man who was in the Civil War "in the name of Artemus Davies . . . strong-minded, very central [single-minded?] in thought and action. Hence the necessity as will be of the training of the direction of the mind and of the developing of same . . ."

This fellow, named in his present incarnation Robin Belote, was born in Selma, Alabama, and had a reading in 1925 at the age of five months. He would take up religious study "as pertaining to psychological and astronomical conditions," said his reading, because he had been influenced by a "heralder of new religious thought" in Arabia in some remote past. Furthermore, he had abilities as a trained mathematician or banker.

From a life in Atlantis when he taught psychology and "the transmission of thought through ether," he would carry over these interests.

At twenty-two, these influences were evident. Cayce's secretary, now married and known as Glady Davis Turner, had followed this child's progress personally, and in 1947 she reported that he was "always an honor student; worked his way through school.

"Very centered in thought and action as a leader and teacher (heralder) in the Seventh Day Adventist religious movement.

"Always made his own way financially; family received help from him in this respect very early. Outstanding in his religious leadership in the Seventh Day Adventist Schools which he attended. Is now a teacher in the school himself. Always good in mathematics.

"Very devoutly interested in 'transmission' of messages from God to old prophets, etc.—a 'heralder' of a return to religion and especially to *his* chosen religion."

Robin eventually obtained his doctor's degree in chemistry and became head of the department at the Seventh Day Adventist College in Nebraska.

"Not of Thyself . . ."

The Law of Karma is not all, however.

This would be a hopeless world if it were, for we would be so bogged down by our accumulation of karmic debt that we would be paying from now on.

There is, to those who choose it, the Law of Grace. "For the Law of the Lord is perfect," explained Cayce, "and whatever an entity, an individual, sows, that must he reap. That as law cannot be changed. As to whether one meets it in the letter of the law or in mercy, in grace, becomes the choice of the entity. If one would have mercy, grace, love, friends, one must show self in such a manner to those with whom one becomes associated. For like begets like.

"There are barriers builded, yes. These may be taken away in Him, Who has paid the price for thee; not of thyself, but in faith, in love, in patience, in kindness, in gentleness may it be met.

"That these have been the experiences [this particular
49

person's ill fortune] may appear to the entity as rather unfair. Is it? The Law of the Lord is perfect. His grace is sufficient, if thy patience will be sufficient also. . . ."

Karma, Cayce told another, is met either in self or in Him. If we commit a sin, or entertain fear, the soul must die. Not in that moment or even that era, but if the soul continues in sin, it is subject to its effects. "But God has not willed that any soul should perish; He has with every temptation prepared a way of escape.

"Hence, He, the Word, the Light, the Truth, came into the earth, paid the price of death, that we through Him might have life more abundantly; eternal life, the consciousness of eternal life, the consciousness of eternity, and that we are one with Him."

At two days, little Alice Luane had no way of protesting her karma. Her reading on April 20, 1933, stated, however, that she would go into the field of vocational training, thus "enabling others to choose their own activity." She would show "high mental abilities," and, her parents were told, "many shall be those influenced by the . . . entity's sojourn through this experience."

She was, strangely, warned of great anxiety which would surround her at about the age of fourteen. This was hardly to be interpreted that she would contract polio, but that's what happened when she reached that age.

"She will make many men step around!" had read her forecast. This was proven true and when she married at twenty-three, her bridegroom carried her down the aisle!

Her high-spirited determination and ability for leadership which her reading foretold served her well as she grew to womanhood and rose above her handicap, which had put her in a wheelchair. When she was eighteen, according to her grandmother's report, Alice was "intending to teach disabled people handicrafts after she leaves school where she is majoring in art. . . . Her reading said she might go in for vocational guidance and I think her work will be very similar to that idea."

After graduation with high honors from junior college at twenty-two, Alice Luane did teach handicapped children and her influence on their destinies was obviously a fact.

In studying the many readings for children and their accompanying reports in later years, one is struck by the number of tragedies which occurred among them. At least two were drowned; there were at least two emotional and mental problems, and Alice Luane was crippled by polio.

Of course, this is partly due to the fact that the children were in tragic straits before being brought to Cayce for help. But if ill-fortune was to strike later, this was never held over their heads. It is characteristic of the Cayce readings that always a sense of optimism, of the possibility of good, prevailed. When trouble loomed, the prediction was tempered by compassion. Thus, Alice's polio perhaps had been foreseen, but in her reading, the parents were merely warned of a bad time for her at fourteen.

Cayce seemed to be treating each case as if it were in the law of Grace that it could be met. Certainly, Alice Luane was a sparkling example of that Law.

Once, in 1952, I attended a lecture by Tom Sugrue only months before his death. He sat in the living room at the old headquarters in his wheelchair, his face lean from pain and great self-discipline, his eyes bright with the wisdom it had taught him. He spoke then of this very subject, the prophecies regarding "The New Age" and the time of the return of Christ. He had suffered for years with crippling arthritis, had triumphed over his infirmities, and was a living demonstration of the virtue by which destiny is carved: patience.

Now he reminded us that we, too, had pain waiting for us in the future, perhaps, and that we had best prepare ourselves for it. It was a jarring reminder that we all err and are under the Law. He explained that karma was sometimes delayed for several lives until we were strong enough to accept it.

"Patience, love, kindness, gentleness, long-suffering, brotherly love. There is no law against any of these," Cayce had said. "For they are the law of consistency in the search for peace . . . they themselves bring peace." In his way, Tom Sugrue had discovered this for himself. He lived to tell about it.

V

ATLANTIS RISING?

"Poseidia (Atlantis) to rise again. Expect it in '68 and '69. Not so far away!" Such was the amazing prediction given on June 28, 1940. Can we count on it? Science has taken a look at Cayce's forecast and has stated the equivalent of "Maybe so!"

It is difficult to believe there ever was such a continent as Atlantis or its Pacific Ocean counterpart, Lemuria. And yet the idea intrigues us, and becomes more believable the more we study the Cayce data.

From the readings we find that a great civilization once existed in the North Atlantic, in the location known as the Sargasso Sea, on a large continent about the size of Europe and Russia combined. Cayce said that it was first populated about ten and one half million years ago, that many upheavals and changes took place during the 200,000 years of its culture, and that it was finally destroyed after three major cataclysms several thousand years apart, the final one being about 10,100 B.C.

In 1958, a highly qualified research geologist* compared Cayce's reading on Atlantis with geologic concepts of the present day, and then compiled a study of this in a pamphlet with a jawbreaker of a title: "A Psychic Interpretation of Some Late Cenozoic Events Compared with Selected Scientific Data." (In later reprintings by the A.R.E. Press, the title became, thank goodness, simply "Earth Changes.")

---

*As he prefers to remain anonymous, he will be identified throughout as "the author of 'Earth Changes'" or as "the Geologist."

This revolutionary study represents a new approach—he has given a new dignity to seemingly farfetched ideas of man and his history.

Science agrees tentatively now that the earth is about five billion years old, and has been changed about many times in its long life. Where there was once ocean, there are now cities. Where there are cities and farms, great fishes once swam. Volcanoes, earthquakes, floods and just plain erosion have shaken up the crust, wrinkled it, smoothed it out, washed it down, and set it out to dry in the sun. In the long process, many species of life have flourished and then become extinct.

Geologists have long known of a vast undersea mountain range in the North Atlantic. When the ocean cable was laid in the late 1870's, a systematic mapping of the area revealed a great mountain chain running north-south through the Atlantic. Lava found in the ocean bed of Atlantic waters dates within the past fifteen thousand years and shows evidence of having cooled *above water*.

Ancient maps indicate continents occupying the Atlantic and Pacific, and archeologists today are discovering artifacts and other evidence of buried cities predating Egypt—for example, the pyramids near Mexico City, judged from the lava found there to be eight thousand years old. Central America and Egypt have similarities of pyramid structure, although separated by the Atlantic. These and other lands apparently survived the last great balancing up of ocean and land, and yield their secrets slowly as science learns how to seek them. Scholars and philosophers have brought to literature a wealth of legend, lore, and speculation on the fabled lands of Atlantis and Lemuria. Plato, Francis Bacon, and the Roman scholar Pliny wrote of them.

Egerton Sykes of England, foremost world authority on the lore of Atlantis, who in 1965 visited Virgina Beach and lectured during the A.R.E. Conference on Atlantis, pointed out that many cultures in the world have "deluge legends." The legend of a great flood that long ago destroyed many lives and inundated the land is common to many peoples, including the American Indians. Belief in the advent of a savior who comes from the East is universal. There are common legends of lands in the Pacific and of a highly advanced race of people, remembered in the lore of China, Greece, South Pacific islands, and South America. If these similarities in religions, architecture, and traditions have existed since ancient times, how did it happen unless there was a common origin of the world's far-flung cultures?

Socrates, as reported in Plato's *Republic,* revealed that in about 590 B.C. the Greek philosopher Solon visited in Egypt and asked the priests there about antiquity. An old priest replied, "There have been, and will be again, many destructions of mankind arising out of many causes; the greatest have been brought about by the agencies of fire and water . . . You remember a single deluge only, but there were many previous ones." He then adds that "there formerly dwelt in your land the fairest and noblest race of man which ever lived, and you and your whole city are descended from a small seed or remnant of them which survived."

The old Egyptian went on to say that at that time the Egyptian constitution was eight thousand years old, while Greece was a thousand years older.

He might have been speaking to us, for we of course "remember a single deluge only"—that which Noah survived and which is recorded in Genesis.

Several thousand books have been written on these last continents. Their authors include Lewis Spence and Colonel James Churchward, the latter claiming to base his several volumes on Mu and its culture on ancient tablets he found in a temple school monastery in India.

To the questions raised from spontaneous references Cayce made from time to time to Atlantean peoples, he gave detailed descriptions of the lost civilization. He said that it occupied the Atlantic, extending to include our eastern seaboard and further, to the Mississippi River. He said that the people were highly developed but degenerated after they misused God's gifts to them, and brought about their own destruction in their later period.

In the age of their enlightenment, they worshipped the One God, using the sun as their symbol of Him. But in her later days of chaos and dispersion, refugees who went into other lands to begin new colonies gradually came to worship the sun itself, as the English colonists found the American Indians doing. Among the Indians, the Iroquois were the direct descendents of the Atlanteans, as were the Mound Builders.

But perhaps America's most significant tie with Atlantis is her character as a nation, which Cayce says resembled theirs as a gifted, scientifically minded, and enterprising people. They were originally a peace-loving people but later were divided into two factions: the "children of the Law of One" and the "Sons of Belial." Atlantean ideals of the Fatherhood of God and the Brotherhood of Man, says Cayce, have been reflected in our own American ideals, perpetuated from the time of Atlantis.

As a nation, they were for long periods a righteous people who discovered the uses of gasses for balloons, and electricity for lighting and heating their homes, for elevators, and one-line cars. They discovered and developed radio and television, and later, air power and aerial photography. They even had amphibian planes which carried them through water and over land.

Finally, they solved the mystery of solar energy conversion, using what Cayce called the "Great Crystal" to harness the sun's energy. This was originally used as a kind of oracle or communication with God, but it could also be used to regenerate the human body, to heal it and otherwise perfect it. Thus, Atlanteans discovered the secret of youth and lived for hundreds of years thereby!

The crystal operated by reflecting the sun to a greater or lesser degree, depending upon how it was "tuned," and could be tuned up to a pitch so devastating that the rays could destroy rather than restore. When those in power forgot their responsibility to use the crystal for good and gained supremacy over the moral elements of the society, the crystal was used destructively. An accidental tuning of it to a high degree brought about volcanic activity in the earth, which led to the final deluge.

After the first destructions about fifteen thousand years before Christ, the nation was no longer one large continent. It had been broken up into five smaller islands, the main ones being Poseidia, Aryan, and Og.

The end of Atlantis was the beginning of Egypt, Greece, and the Incas. This would corroborate the statement of the Egyptian priest in *The Republic* dating his nation and that of Greece at around eight or nine thousand years B.C.

At the time of Atlantis, there existed also the older continent of Lemuria. This one sank beneath the Pacific before Atlantis' downfall, under similar conditions. It was another highly civilized land, the survivors of which established a new culture in America and Mexico, perpetuating their ancient religious concepts very much as the Atlanteans perpetuated theirs in the Mediterranean.

Harking back to the beginnings of man's history, even before Atlantis, Cayce gives us a picture of what the earth was like ten and one half *million* years ago, when the poles were changed around to make what is now frigid, tropical. He says that the Sahara and Gobi deserts were fertile, prosperous lands in the first days of human life on earth. He identified Iran as the Garden of Eden referred to in Genesis. In America the Mississippi basin was an ocean bed. In the west, only the "plateau" of Nevada, Utah, and Arizona was above water, the rest apparently having been ocean bed, also. The Atlantic seaboard was the Atlantean lowlands. The Ural Mountains were tropical, as was Siberia and Hudson Bay! The Nile River then emptied into the Atlantic.

In his study of the psychic data of Edgar Cayce, the Geologist wrote that he found the readings both logical and consistent. He studied fifty readings, twenty of which describe events of earth history that occurred ten million years B.C. or since then. He said that some of these agree, others disagree, with present scientific concepts.

He then pointed out that recent scientific research, such as deep-sea, paleomagnetic, and that on the absolute age of geologic materials (e.g. radiocarbon dating) have tended to render the readings *more probable*.

He further points out that recently maps thought to be "many thousands of years old" have been discovered in Greenland, Antarctica and other portions of the world. They are highly accurate, he says, showing mountain ranges which have since been found by the Army Map Service. What is the more remarkable, he says, is that they show both Greenland and Antarctica in an unglaciated state. (This seems to agree with Cayce's views of a tropical Arctic and Antarctic.)

He adds that expeditions to Greenland and Antarctica

have since verified the mountainous topography beneath the ice, by means of seismic surveys. He points out that the authority who solved the map projections, A. H. Mallory, "thinks it possible that the ancient cartographers . . . might have accomplished their feats by mapping from the air."

The Geologist then cites many more favorable comparisons between Cayce's views and scientific discoveries of recent date. In addition to the maps cited above, there have been findings that support Cayce's assertion that the temperatures were different from what they are today.

The date of Stonehenge in England has been found to be about 1848 B.C. and was referred to by Cayce as having been built by refugees from the Holy Land when it was sacked by the Chaldeans and Persians.

The Geologist also suggests that a discovery made in 1958 of a unified field theory which relates mass, energy, and gravity, may bear out a 1932 Cayce prediction that in 1958 the secret of how the Great Pyramid of Gizeh was built would be discovered.

Such events, says the Geologist, lead us to think that "it is no longer necessary to accept some psychic statements on faith alone."

There are new techniques of determining the ages of organic substances rich in carbon by means of radiocarbon dating. Geologists can test the contents of the stomach of a mammoth pried from frigid Siberian wastelands; they can take "cores" of the ocean bed materials beneath several miles of water and can determine the ages of the various layers of the ocean floors and their geologic history. They can tell the temperature at which ancient shells grew 200 million years ago! With such tools, the story of Atlantis does seem to have some chance of being told with ever-increasing accuracy by science.

Other readings given in the 1930's and '40's tell of *future* geologic changes which Cayce says will take place in the earth. One of the most startling predictions is that Atlantis will rise once again, first to be seen in the Bahamas where is located that submerged continent's highest land areas. Here, southwest of the island of Bimini, specifically, is where we can expect it in 1968 or 1969!

There will be a shifting of the poles so that "where there

have been [temperatures] of a frigid or semi-tropical will become the more tropical, and moss and fern will grow." Climate changes and final shifting of the poles will occur approximately forty years after geologic disturbances first in the South Pacific and in the Mediterranean. The volcanoes Vesuvius and Pelee are also mentioned in connection with trouble in California and Nevada, which will follow their eruptions.

Disturbances will be felt throughout the world, but particularly in the western part of America, in the eastern New York state area, in Japan, northern Europe, and the Arctic and Antarctic. Land will appear both in the Atlantic and in the Pacific, and there will be oceans and bays where there is now land.

The standard geologic concept of earth change is that it takes place slowly over long periods of time, the Geologist states. He adds that "the large number of 'catastrophic' events predicted for the period from 1958 to 2001 A.D. are out of harmony with this concept of gradual change."

He confirms tendencies toward the possible fulfillment of the Cayce predictions, in pointing out the worldwide earth events that have been taking place in recent years. The waters of the North Altantic are warming up. It's getting warmer around the poles, and since 1900 the thickness of the polar icecap in the Arctic has decreased by three feet. A new pattern of hurricanes which strike inland as never before adds to the list. These changes, which include rising and sinking of land and more frequent volcanic eruptions, indicate something could be happening to our earth that will have a bearing on future conditions.

Upheavals!

By 1932, Cayce said, the changes in the earth would begin to be evident, at the same time that a change occured in the consciousness of mankind as we entered the Aquarian Age.

In 1936 there would be catastrophe in the form of great political changes "that will make different *maps* of the world." The very earth would be disturbed, as there would be a shifting of the interior of the earth in relation-

58

ship to the poles. There would be upheavals in the earth's interior and wars in the affairs of men.

This was given on February 8, 1932, in answer to a request that Cayce "forecast the principal events for the next fifty years affecting the welfare of the human race."

"This had best be cast after the great catastrophe that's coming to the world in '36," replied Cayce, "in the form of the breaking up of many *powers* that now exist as factors in the world affairs. . . . Then, with the breaking up in '36 will be the *changes* that will make different maps of the world." (See pp. 85-88.)

A later question in another reading was: "What will be the type and extent of the upheaval in '36?"

"The wars, the upheavals in the interior of the earth, and the shifting of same by the differentiation in the axis as respecting the positions from the Polaris center," was the answer.

In August of 1932 someone asked if there were to be physical changes in the earth's surface in Alabama, which seemed to be a kind of testing for more specific and localized predictions. The answer was affirmative.

"When will the changes begin?" was asked.

"Thirty-six to thirty-eight," was the answer.

"What part of the state will be affected?"

"The northwestern part and the extreme southwestern part."

In November, Alabama's future was again predicted, when Cayce was asked if that state's physical changes were to be sudden, or gradual. The answer was "Gradual." They would take the form of sinking and inundations.

There is no doubt that if there had been time enough, in the crowded schedule of readings Cayce was committed to give, that he could have gone over the entire globe with a fine-tooth comb and described the physical changes of every section. However, specific predictions were given for larger areas, and these are next described.

Major Earth Changes Prophecies

The major earth changes prophecies cover a period of sixty-two years, from 1936 to 1998. The changes were to begin in a gradual way and become more pronounced beginning in 1968 or 1969.

They were to come about by earthquakes and volcanic action, sinking and rising of land, flooding of some lands and rechanneling of existing waterways. Some lands would be devastated, others would be perfectly safe. Coasts were to fall away or be inundated, leaving new coastlines.

Major earthquakes and other natural disasters have been recorded over the centuries. They include the city of Lisbon, Portugal, which in 1755 was engulfed by ocean waves created by an earthquake which killed up to 60,000 people. In 1811-1812 a new lake, Reelfoot, was formed in Tennessee and Kentucky, when part of the Mississippi floodplain sank. In Japan, the cities of Tokyo and Yokohama, Mino and Owari have been destroyed or greatly damaged by quakes since 1897. Other countries have suffered similar disasters—in India four major quakes have occurred since 1897. In that year, they were so severe that thirty lakes appeared in Bengal and Assam.

Certain regions of the world have earthquake "faults" or breaks in rock strata, and contain the world's active volcanoes. Seismologists report around eight thousand earth disturbances annually throughout the world. Japan lies astride the great Pacific rim earthquake belt, and has a number of faults, making it highly susceptible to major disturbances.

This earthquake belt borders the Pacific along the western edge of the Great Basin, extending along the coasts of North and South America and the eastern coast of Japan. Here are located the East Indian and West Indian islands and the islands of the Pacific. Other earthquake regions are the Mediterranean coastal areas of Italy and Greece, and the Himalayas.

So earthquakes were certainly not new when Cayce forecast big changes for the second half of the century: They were occurring along with other lesser forces that alter the topography. The year 1936, in fact, was not the first time in earth's history to see the shifting of the poles, according to Cayce.

This is challenged by science, which in general maintains that the continents and poles have remained in position throughout the history of the globe.

There is, however, the "continental drift" theory which holds that the continents drifted apart and are still slowly moving farther and farther from each other. Some think that the poles have shifted in past geologic times, creating opposites in climate conditions. One group of scientists seeks to explain the glaciation that is known to have taken place in India, South America, South Africa, and Australia at one time by assuming that the North Pole had then been in the vicinity of Hawaii. Then, the arctic climate would have been centered around the North Pacific.

Cayce spoke in his readings of "the turning of the axis" and the "changing of the poles" around 50,772 years ago! In this connection he told also of a strange event which occurred at that time involving the problem of "enormous animals" in Atlantis. He stated that nature took a hand and in the changing of the poles, with the sudden change in temperatures, the animals were destroyed by ice.

According to the author of "Earth Changes," as science interprets this, the north pole shifted from a position outside the Arctic Ocean to its present position inside this ocean, thus initiating the ice age described. It is a hypothesis which in 1958 was presented by the scientists Ewing and Donn, he says. It was anticipated by Cayce fourteen years earlier.

The earth changes as forecast by Cayce are as follows:

SOUTH PACIFIC: The changes will begin to be apparent "when there is the first breaking up of some conditions in the South Sea (that's South Pacific, to be sure) and those as apparent in the sinking or rising of that which is almost opposite it, or in the Mediterranean, and the Aetna (Etna) area. Then we may know it has begun."

THE ATLANTIC: "Lands will appear in the Atlantic as well as in the Pacific." "And Poseidia will be among the first portions of Atlantis to rise again. Expect it in sixty-eight or sixty-nine. Not so far away!"

THE PACIFIC: "Lands will appear . . . ." "The greater portion of Japan must go into the sea."

EUROPE: "The upper portion of Europe will be changed as in the twinkling of an eye. . . ." "Even many of the battlefields of the present [1941] will be ocean, will be the seas, the bays, the lands over which the new order will carry on their trade as one with another."

AMERICA: "All over the country many physical changes of a minor or greater degree. The greater change will be in the North Atlantic Seaboard. Watch New York, Connecticut and the like.

"Many portions of the East Coast will be disturbed, as well as many portions of the West Coast, as well as the central portion of the United States.

"Los Angeles, San Francisco, most all of these will be among those that will be destroyed before New York, even.

"Portions of the now east coast of New York, or New York City itself, will in the main disappear. This will be another generation, though, here; while the southern portions of Carolina, Georgia, these will disappear. This will be much sooner.

"The waters of the Great Lakes will empty into the Gulf of Mexico.

"If there are greater activities in Vesuvius or Pelee, then the southern coast of California—and the areas between Salt Lake and the southern portions of Nevada—may expect, within three months following same, an inundation caused by the earthquakes.

"Safety lands will be the area around Norfolk, Virginia Beach, parts of Ohio, Indiana, and Illinois and much of the southern portion of Canada and the eastern portion of Canada."

ARCTIC AND ANTARCTIC: "There will be upheavals in the Arctic and the Antarctic that will make for the eruptions of volcanoes in the Torrid areas, and there will be the shifting then of the poles—so that where there have been those of a frigid or semi-tropical will become the more tropical, and moss and fern will grow . . ."

SEALANES: "Strifes will arise throughout the period. Watch for them near the Davis Straits, where there will be attempts to keep open a life line to a land.

"Watch for them in Libya and in Egypt, and in Syria. Through the straits around those areas above Austrialia; in the Indian Ocean and the Persian Gulf.

"Ye say that these are of the sea. Yes, for there will be the breaking up, until the time where there are people in every land who will say that this or that shows the hand of divine interference—or that nature is taking a hand—or that this or that is the natural consequence of good judgments . . ."

GENERAL: "The earth will be broken up in many places. The early portion will see a change in the physical aspect of the west coast of America. There will be open waters appearing in the northern portions of Greenland. There will be new lands seen off the Caribbean Sea, and dry land will appear . . . South America shall be shaken up from the uppermost portion to the end, and in the Antarctic off Tierra del Fuego, land, and a strait with rushing waters . . ."

The shifting of the poles as a logical consequence of large scale crustal displacements, according to the Geologist, will be due much later. According to Cayce, this will occur around the year 2,000 to 2,001.

But it will begin with the signs in the South Pacific and the Mediterranean which Cayce describes, and the appearance of land near Bimini. The West Coast destruction will be early on this time clock of events, as will the inundations of parts of the Carolinas and Georgia.

To show how unlikely is the safety of relatively high ground when this begins is the example of Norfolk, which was told it would remain a good place to be even though it is low and close to the sea. "Norfolk is to be a mighty good place, and a safe place when turmoils are to arise," one person was told; "Though it may appear that it may be in the line of those areas to rise, while many a higher land will sink. This is a good area to stick to."

More Scientific Observations

"How soon will the changes in the earth's activity begin to be apparent?" one person wanted to know in 1932.

"The indications are that some of these have already begun," Cayce said. "yet others would say that these are only temporary. We would say they have begun."

The Earthquake Information Bulletin of the National Earthquake Information Center (NEIC) states: "The strongest earthquake ever located in this area [Mississippi] occurred December 16, 1931." This brings to mind that Mississippi and its general locale has never been an earthquake center but has had three quakes in recent history, the

63

third occurring in June, 1967. Thus, for that state, something new is going on. It could be what Cayce was referring to. Other areas have increased in earthquake activity since 1932, according to the *Bulletin* of the Seismological Society of America (Vol. 57, No. 3) for June, 1967: "There appears to be an increase of larger intensity and magnitude earthquakes since 1936 in Washington State, and especially in the Puget Sound area since 1949."

Strangely, the year 1932 marked the beginning of a program by the Coast and Geodetic Survey to record accurately earth motions in the seismically active regions of the western United States. "Fortunately this was done in time to record the notable 1933 Long Beach, California and 1935 Helena, Montana earthquakes," states the NEIC *Bulletin.* "These provided the first data of destructive ground motions for engineering applications, and an impetus for strong motions studies."

In 1936 the Seismological Field survey was established to carry out earthquake investigations in the western United States.

The June, 1967, issue, of the *Bulletin* reveals that nearly a million lives have been claimed by earthquakes in this century alone. Bahngrell Brown, in an article entitled "Geology of Disaster" *(The Professional Geologist,* November, 1966), estimated that since the time of Christ, five million lives have been lost by natural cataclysms. From this, it would seem that earth activities are increasing in severity.

Brown is interested in geology's potential ability to *predict* earthquakes and other disasters of natural forces, allowing evacuation of endangered masses of people to safe ground. His thinking in regard to the imminence of a major change is markedly in line with the Cayce predictions. "It may be noted that the spacing of these events over the last one hundred years would suggest that sacrifice in life is imminent.

"As we face the future, we might let our imaginations dwell on the likelihood of these long-overdue possibilities for that future:

"1. A Crater Lake type eruption in the belt of the "dormant" U.S. volcanoes.

"2. A recurrence of the terrible 1811-12 earthquake in

the Mississippi Valley, where there are now great cities."

"3.   An unlikely (but possible) tsunami in the Gulf of Mexico.

"4.   Any mountain city in an avalanche path."*

A major seismic disturbance now seems about to occur in the area of the San Andreas fault, according to scientists. It is a trench six hundred miles long running along the coast of California, with many branches cutting into wider areas to the east of it. The earthquakes of 1906, 1957, and 1838 were the largest which have happened there in recent times.

Active earthquake regions have mainly been in the western part of the United States and Alaska and so we are not alarmed at statistics concerning that section.

What does alarm geologists is the fact that for the past several years the usually rumbling San Andreas Fault has grown quiet—too quiet, and they fear that it may be building up for real trouble.

The year 1966 was a "dry" year for earthquakes, according to Jerry L. Coffman, who in the March, 1967, NEIC *Bulletin* states: "We have not had a 'great' earthquake since the Good Friday shock of March 28, 1964, in Alaska, and only one other—on October 13, 1963, in the remote Kurile Islands north of Japan—since the May, 1960, earthquake in Chile. . . .

"Does this mean we are about to have several great earthquakes? Not necessarily. We may complete an unprecedented fourth year without a great earthquake, or a single great event may occur at any time. Earthquakes are not yet predictable."

The August, 1967, *Bulletin* says, "Statistics developed over the first half of this century indicate that about one great earthquake will occur annually on the average." Even major shocks are absent, it adds, in recent years. "Most seismologists believe that strain is constantly increasing until released by an earthquake. If this is true, then it is only a question of time—and where—until the next 'great' shock strikes."

*Quoted by permission of the American Institute of Professional Geologists.

Japan is the most seismically active nation in the world. Again, we wrote the NEIC *Bulletin* for March, 1967: "An unusual earthquake swarm has been experienced by the people of Matsushiro, Japan, a town of 22,000 inhabitants about one hundred miles northwest of Tokyo. It all began August 3, 1965, and is still continuing.

"The inhabitants of Matsushiro are quite familiar with earthquakes, but the continuous shakings which have awakened them throughout the night for months and caused them to take to the open fields at times for refuge are something different. Some have said that the 'gods' are angry because instruments were set up near the shrine on Mount Minakami, the focal point of the shocks.

"From August, 1965, to December, 1966, over 565,000 earthquakes were recorded, with about 59,000 of these strong enough to be felt. On April 17, alone, 6,780 shocks were recorded and 661 were felt. Three hundred homes were damaged on this date as the repeated shaking continued to reduce buildings and walls to rubble. . . .

"There is no conclusive evidence of the cause of these earthquakes. One theory is that molten rock is pushing up toward the now dormant Minakami volcano. But would this explain the alteration of the surrounding landscape? Highly sensitive instruments have indicated a very slight rising and tilting of the mountains east of Matsushiro and a sinking of the valley floor. Still another theory relates these observations to tectonic (mountain-building) forces.

"This series of earthquakes has subsided somewhat, to 7,371 in December. Meanwhile, the residents of Matsushiro still live an uneasy life. Some think the shocks will eventually cease, but the less optimistic believe the earth is building up to an eventual major blow-up."

Disturbances that lead to earth changes include volcanic action, which scientists have observed have been on the increase since 1947. According to Cayce, the first breaking up was to happen in the Pacific area and a check by the author of "Earth Changes" shows increased activity in the Hawaiian Islands since 1958; a violent eruption on Bali in 1963; and a new volcano being built over the shattered remains of Krakatoa (blown apart in 1883). North of Auckland, Rumble III, a volcanic island, was violently active in November and December of 1964.

In the Pacific, the Alaskan earthquake in 1964 was preceded by the appearance in November, 1963, of a volcanic island off Iceland, called Surtsey, near the Arctic Circle. According to "Earth Changes," "Recent measurements of crustal upwarping in the Canadian Arctic, Spitsbergen, and Greenland show relatively rapid rates of uplift—believed due to unloading by recently vanished or presently melting ice masses."

Volcanic activity has also been stepped up in the Atlantic, particularly in the Azores, site of the Atlantis mainland. A paper by F. Machado presented at the IAV Symposium on Volcanology (New Zealand) in November, 1965, entitled "Activity of the Atlantic Volcanoes, 1947-1965," points out that "since 1947 volcanic activity increased considerably in the oceanic volcanoes of the Atlantic." He adds that "eruptions were reported first in Iceland, and then successively in the Canaries, the Cape Verde Islands, the Azores, Tristan da Cunha, and again in Iceland, where an eruption is still going on (June, 1965)."

He goes on to state that Hekla in Iceland had been quiescent since 1913. On March 29, 1947, a new eruption started, causing a huge cloud to be carried to Finland by high atmospheric winds. Lava flooded the area, and the activity lasted for thirteen months. In 1961, a new Iceland eruption occurred, and an explosive submarine eruption off the coast began in 1963. In 1964 it "became effusive and continued thus until May, 1965."

Earthquakes preceded similar eruption on September 27, 1957, off Fayal Island, Azores, when a new sand isthmus was formed to the main island, states the report.

On May 30, 1967, the Associated Press reported that the four mouths of the volcano on Stromboli Island, Messina, Sicily, "have fused into a single lava-spouting crater lake three hundred yards across. This occurred over a fifty-day period of eruptions, with lava flowing down to the sea at safe distances from fishing villages."

The Etna area (mentioned by Cayce as an important area which will be active at the beginning of earth changes) is an active volcano of historic renown. It exploded in 1960, and in 1964 experienced its most violent eruption in ten years. It is not so much the volcanic activity which will signal other major earth disturbances, then, but the sinking or rising of the area around it.

The author of "Earth Changes" suggests that Cayce's "perplexing statement about the *sinking* or *rising* in the Mediterranean area may possibly be connected with the recent water-level drop in Greek harbors. The drop would indicate *rising* of the land in this eastern part of the Mediterranean."

He quotes a Reuters dispatch from Athens which describes the drop in 1959 as being more than three feet in many places, causing small boats to sit on the sea bottom. The condition remained; and scientists cannot explain what caused it.

Lest we underestimate the power of the 1964 Alaskan earthquake, we have the report in the *Virginian Pilot* (November 12, 1967) that it literally moved mountains! It also temporarily raised the level of the Mississippi River, and sent a seismic wave as far as the Antarctic!

"The [Commerce] Department's Coast and Geodetic Survey, more than three years after the Good Friday disaster, is still gathering data on the effects of the strongest earthquake ever recorded on the North American continent," states this Associated Press story.

"Some of its findings are incorporated in a technical report issued by the Environmental Science Services Administration.

"It said some Alaskan mountains subsided because of the quake, the sea floor in one area rose as much as fifty feet, and a seismic wave was recorded in the Antarctic 22½ hours after the quake.

"This giant wave, the report said, had traveled 8,445 miles at 430 miles an hour.

"The earthquake caused one hundred thirty-one deaths and more than $750 million in damage not only in Alaska but along the U.S. Pacific coast as well.

"Here are some findings from the report:

"Mountains on Kodiak Island and the Kenai Peninsula and the Chugach Mountains near Prince William Sound subsided seven feet or more. Earlier surveys revealed that some Kenai Peninsula Mountains shifted laterally about five feet.

"The ocean floor rose in an area 480 miles by 127 miles with the highest upheaval fifty feet—the biggest ever recorded—between Kodiak and Montague Islands.

"Shocks waves oscillated the water as far away as Key West, 3,968 miles distant. Surges of water began along the Gulf Coast of Louisiana and Texas between thirty and forty minutes after the quake."

On Tuesday, December 5, 1967, South America was again in the news, this time because of a volcano erupting on the Antarctic island of Deception. This is in the area of Tierra del Fuego, just to the north of the Antarctic Peninsula. As Cayce predicted, "South America shall be shaken up from the uppermost portion to the end, and in the Antarctic off Tierra del Fuego, *land*, and a strait with rushing waters. . . .

"There will be upheavals in the Arctic and the Antarctic that will make for the eruptions of volcanoes in the Torrid areas. . . ."

This particular eruption came "from the depths of an ancient lake on the island, and wrecked the scientific bases of three nations, forcing researchers to flee, according to Chilean officials. Braving a rain of ashes and rocks, Chilean navy helicopters took thirty Chilean and eight British researchers and military personnel to the Chilean ship *Piloto Pardo* waiting off shore.

"An Argentine group of fourteen was to be taken off by the Argentine ship *Bahia Aguirre,* the Chilean navy said.

"No volcanic eruption had been reported in more than 120 years on the island until geysers of boiling water from the lake began shooting up several days ago.

"Then the volcano erupted in full fury Monday, sending ash and rock into the air and sending lava down ravines from the lake. A dense cloud of smoke shrouded the island and ashes blanketed the white ice caps.

"The Interior Ministry said the British, Chilean, and Argentine bases, hewn from the bitterly cold wastes, were wrecked by the volcano's force. The bases are used for weather and oceanographic research.

"A Chilean navy spokesman said helicopters had to be used to bring off the Chileans and Britons because rough waters and the eruption of ashes and stones made it impossible to use boats.

" 'We shall not be returning to the island until we know it is completely safe,' said a British spokesman."

VI

PEOPLE RISING!

God has taken his place in the divine council;
in the midst of the gods he holds judgment:
'How long will you judge unjustly and show partiality
  to the wicked?'
'Give justice to the weak and the fatherless;
maintain the right of the afflicted and the destitute.
Rescue the weak and the needy:
  deliver them from the hand of the wicked.'

They have neither knowledge nor understanding,
  they walk about in darkness;
  all the foundations of the earth are shaken.

I say, 'You are gods,
  sons of the Most High, all of you:
Nevertheless, you shall die like men,
  and fall like any prince.'

Arise, O God, judge the earth;
  for to thee belong all the nations!

—Psalms 82

On July 26, 1967, as the Detroit riots were in progress
for the fourth consecutive day, I was in the midst of researching the Cayce files on race relations. I found the
readings chillingly immediate—they could have been
uttered during the long, hot summer of '67 instead of that
far-off summer nearly thirty years ago.

During the time this book was being written, in fact,

70

much has happened that was directly related to the readings' picture of this era. Most dramatic and obvious were the racial conflicts which Edgar Cayce predicted, pointing out that this was the way men took "when there is the plenty in some areas and a lack . . . in the life of others."

Unless, in fact, we remembered that we are indeed our brother's keeper, there would be a revolution in this country and "a dividing of the sections one against another.

"Ye are to have a division in thine own land before there is the second of the Presidents that next will not live through his office—a mob rule!"

"Unless there is, then, a more universal oneness of purpose on the part of all, this will one day bring—here—in America—revolution!" (June, 1939)

He laid America's problems for these times. to her "unbelief." In 1943 he delineated the errors and their results for us "today," meaning the period that included that time and this, old problems which have festered over the years, stemming from centuries past.

"The ideals, the purposes that called the nation into being are well," he said. "It might be answered by saying that there needs to be on the part of each man, each woman, the adhering to those principles that caused the formulating of the American thought.

"Yet in the present there are seen many complex problems, many conditions that are variance to the First Cause (God) or first principles, not only among groups and individuals in high places, both from the political and the economic situations, but the problems of labor-capital, as well. As all of these are problems in America today, as well as that of religious thought, religious principles, racial concern—which are mass as well as individual and group thought. . . .

"To meet same? Only that each soul turns not to self alone and cry for strength, but that each soul lives in such a manner that there may be the awakening to the needs, the purposes, the causes for the nation coming into existence!

"That such is, and is to be, a part of the experience of America is because of unbelief!"

The riots were met with horror and acknowledgment of wrongs long existent, mingled with the soul-searching which Cayce predicted when he advised that "each soul lives in such a manner that there may be the awakening to the . . . purposes for the nation coming into existence." This was countered by the die-hard expressions that will not quite let these people go. There was emotion and hard thinking and a genuine effort on both sides to do something, and do it now. There were the stirrings of the old cry "Am I my brother's keeper?" and the answer, from pulpits, streetcorners, homes, and many groups was "Yes!"

Edgar Cayce never condoned the riots, crime, revolution which he warned about. He merely predicted them, saying that these were the natural result of injustice. He said that conditions as they have been over the years just could not go on.

On November 22, 1963, I was on the staff of the A.R.E. and remember the anguish of that day and the awe we felt that another prophecy had been fulfilled. As in offices all over the nation, we gathered around a radio and listened to the strained and conflicting reports that President Kennedy had been shot. Then we heard the terrible news that he was dead.

We looked at one another in shocked amazement. "Edgar Cayce predicted this," we reminded ourselves. Franklin Roosevelt had been the *first* president to die in office since 1939, when the prophecy was given: "Ye are to have a division in thine own land before there is the second of the Presidents that next will not live through his office—a mob rule!"

John F. Kennedy was "the second of the Presidents."

The readings of Edgar Cayce are for all people. However, their message for the New Age is meant no more for the extreme rabble-rousers, the lawbreakers, than it is for the "status quo." It is for all those who are sincerely trying to use their talents, understanding, knowledge, position, and money—in harmony with the laws of God and man—for the constructive goals of mankind, which President Kennedy so well crystallized during his brief tenure in office.

In 1937, Cayce predicted that there was to be a "new awakening" in many portions of the earth.

The social revolution which has been going on since that time is a part of the new awakening, we think, and it refers to that in Africa, South America, and many other continents and nations which are shaking free from colonialism of the past.

Ahead of time, and the times, was this statement given as to our rightful attitude toward all people: "Whoever, wherever he is, that bears the imprint of the Maker in the earth, be he black, white, gray, or grizzled, be he young, be he Hottentot, or on the throne or in the President's chair—all that are in the earth today are thy brothers!"

During the 1920's, a group of idealists asked Cayce how to build a "great society" (although they did not use that term) such as is the goal under President Johnson today. They wanted to build "a world organization" which would ensure hospitals, churches, schools, farm loans, rural road construction, for the underprivileged people of the earth, for the "upbuilding of mankind."

This, said Cayce, has been the dream of many people in times past, who have had much more to work with than did the friends of Cayce. "Same was the idea of Alexander when he sought to conquer the world"—yet he forgot his high purpose which had been bred into him by Aristotle.

"In the tenets of the Christ" may such a plan be brought to realization most successfully. It would take the old-fashioned virtues of faith, hope, love, to bring about the conditions necessary to build a social structure in which people might then help themselves.

An oustanding example of modern progress toward this goal is the Alliance for Progress in South America.

This organization was inaugurated under President Kennedy in 1961, with twenty American nations signing the Charter of Punta del Este. United States aid to these countries was pledged and now, seven years later, a vast business boom and a program for road building, education, and hospitals has been established. Political despotism has been replaced with democratic elections. College students have gone to work in their own poverty-stricken areas to teach the people new skills. The success of the Alliance, which is yearly becoming more effective, has elbowed out Communism, which once threatened these neighbors.

The "awakening" goes on in many places, filling many needs. In not only the Americas, but in India, Africa, illiteracy is being tackled by the teaching programs of many agencies. And in the ghettos, boys and girls are given opportunities to develop many skills under trained supervision. There is a stirring among the impoverished and the low in every corner of the world, and a rising to a common level.

"The leveling must come," Cayce predicted.

Edgar Cayce attributed the division in this country to "fear on the part of those who control capital investment" and a lack of universal oneness of purpose.

Economic Changes Predicted

On the night of March 3, 1929, Gerald Bailey dreamed that he and his friends in the stockbroking business "ought to sell everything, including the box stock."

"A bull seemed to follow Doris Morrow's red dress. . . ."

Cayce was asked to interpret this dream. It was, he said, a key to the stock market situation and should certainly be heeded because he had dreamed correctly. On March 6, Gerald asked for a fuller interpretation. The bull, he learned, was the bull market, of course. "The red indicating the danger in the bull market, yet—as seen—there will still be the continued attempt to keep the market a bull market.

"Hence, we will have a mixture, but gradually sliding off, as seen in the present . . . though this . . . whole condition may change . . . This issue being between those of the reserves of nations and of *individuals* and will cause, unless another of the more stable banking conditions come to the relief—a great disturbance in financial circles. . . ."

On October 29, less than seven months later, the crash occurred. Another of Cayce's interpretations of a prophetic dream was confirmed.

More may come as disturbances to America from within than from without, Cayce said in 1941. This was true. After the war, labor and racial frictions mounted.

But before that, the Depression which followed the crash was the all-consuming world dilemma and for this, he had both immediate and far-reaching predictions. Just before Christmas, 1930, when a bleak Yule was in store for millions, came the question: "When will economic conditions throughout the United States be improved and the present depression be at an end?"

"Beginning with the spring [1931] there will be, in various portions of the country, a change in economic conditions. Another year [1932] will bring those of a greater disturbance in many centers. Then, unless there is the adoption of other conditions, a still greater disturbance in this present land. Then, '34 or '35, things will gradually adjust themselves to the uphill, as it were, for the general conditions."

The Depression deepened in 1931. As Cayce had forecast, the world-wide disturbance reached its lowest point in 1932.

In January of that year, Edgar Cayce was questioned about the Depression's cause and the time the nation could expect a return to normalcy.

"The United States may not expect to recover sooner than any other nation unless its basis for recovery is founded in that that brings peace, harmony, and understanding. As it, the U.S. (in the present) is the leading nation in attempting to give an understanding of the principles of 'Thou shalt love thy neighbor as thyself'; it stands above all others in its financial, in its social positions in the world; yet it has faltered, and—as of old—when troubles arise, when fearful conditions beset thee, the same answer was of old 'Know ye that *sin* lieth at *thy* door!"

That same year, 1931, he said that depressions and good years come and go in cycles of about twenty-four to twenty-five years. The last one had occurred in 1907. Although he did not give the date, we have since lived through another low period that of 1954, termed a "recession" and occurring right on time.

The causes of the Great Depression were different, he said, from those of other times, for they were the "combination of wrath, oppression, and sin."

In November, 1939, he told a labor-management mediator that general changes in financial structures in America were to come about. He said that a greater stabilization of currencies would be needed with the general international conditions, and that it would happen in early summer of the following year. These must be the basic conditions of capital as related to the individual or personal finance, and as to the Government, he added.

An economist asked in June, 1943, "What could our own country be doing toward equalizing opportunities for trade among the nations immediately following the war?"

He answered, "In some quarters, too much is being done already! These are the things over which many disputes will arise. But there must come some basis for an economic situation in all lands, in those that are a part of the united effort against . . . aggression . . . as well as those devastated by war."

This reading went on to say that we would move toward a lowered tariff in many directions, and that it was not only possible to raise the economic standards of the world, but it *must* be done if there was to be a lasting peace.

He likened social ills to cancer cells that rebel, causing destruction.

Although it would take a long time to establish, he predicted an international stabilization of exchange values and said that "there may indeed be another war over just such conditions."

In 1944 he said that there would be many economic changes after World War II and that there will be "more and more upsetting in the monetary units of the land."

The depression of the thirties turned in the forties to inflation and a rising cost of living, thus general instability. According to L.V. Chandler's *Economics of Money and Banking* (New York: Harper and Row, 1964) bank failures and closing of other types of financial institutions led to the adoption since the 1930's of better practices, including better regulations of financial institutions and procedures, insurance of mortgages, Federal Home Loan Banks, etc. There were "many economic changes," as Cayce had predicted, including these and the rise in employment and many shifts in the economy. The peak year of 1948 was followed by a mild recession year, and were followed by quick recovery. Easy and tight money followed each other during those years of ever increasing prices.

Concerning the prediction that a change in our whole financial structure would come about, let us again turn to Chandler: "The whole structure of financial institutions in the United States has undergone tremendous changes since

1914. Perhaps most striking has been the rise of institutions sponsored in one way or another by the federal government: For example, the whole complex of farm-credit institutions, the many new institutions in the housing-credit field, and the Small Business Administration. . . .

"Private financial institutions other than commercial banks have also undergone great changes. Among these are the phenomenal growth in the number and resources of savings-and-loan associations, the rapid growth of credit unions in some areas, the greater aggressiveness of mutual savings banks, the rise and rapid growth of pension funds, and so on."

He cites the decline in banks and their absorption into mergers.

Cayce's prediction of an international stabilization of exchange values is still in the future. Says Chandler: "The international reserve system and international monetary policies have not yet approached a final stage of evolution. The International Monetary Fund has been highly useful, and it continues to grow in usefulness and prestige. But its policies are still undergoing change, especially those relating to the terms and conditions under which it will make its resources available. . . ."

Many questions need to be answered and many financial problems will arise, it is pointed out, before this will become fully workable.

Cayce told us, "These questions [of stabilization of currencies] must be the *basic* conditions of capital as related to the individual and as to the Governments . . ." But the fear of financial woes might be corrected by a return to the trust in God.

Authors William and Paul Paddock have recently predicted worldwide famine which only the United States will be able to alleviate effectively.* This emphasizes Edgar Cayce's warnings of "hardships" and "extreme periods" regarding future food supply. The time ascribed for this could be that generally predicted by Cayce in 1943 for land upheavals "in the next generation."

Back in 1943, Edgar Cayce was asked by a Norfolk resi-

*Famine-1975! (New York: Little, Brown, 1967).

dent if the purchase of a farm in the region between Washington and Norfolk was still advisable. Cayce replied that it was advisable "because of hardships which have not begun yet in this country, so far as the supply and demand for foods is concerned."

To another at that time, he said, "Anyone who can buy a farm is fortunate and buy it if you don't want to grow hungry in some days to come."

"Should I hold the twenty-five acres of land near Oceana (Va.); also, two sites in Linkhorn Park and lots on 54th Street (Virginia Beach, Va.)?" Cayce was asked by still a third person.

"Hold them until at least the early spring; that is, the lots," Cayce advised. "*Hold* the acreage. for that may be the basis for the extreme periods through which all portions of the country must pass—for production for self as well as those closer associated with the body."

Still another reference to the "return to the soil" was made as early as 1938: "All that is for the sustenance of life *is* produced from the soil. Then there must be a return to the soil. Every man must be in that position that he at least creates, by his activities, that which will sustain the body—from the soil; or where he is supplying same to those activities that bring such experiences into the lives of all."

In June, 1938, the Works Progress Administration and the Civilian Conservation Corps had provided many people with jobs. A typical paycheck was $17.50 a week—yet it meant the difference between going hungry and having food to eat.

There were all kinds of projects involving many construction laborers, as well as projects employing destitute people in the arts. Symphony orchestras, writers' workshops and art classes enriched communities wherever they appeared.

But Cayce advocated the "return to the land" all over the country, and "not so much of the makeshift of labor in various fields . . . for unless this comes, there must and will come disruption, turmoil, and strife."

In addition to the population explosion of this age, and the many long-standing economic causes of poverty and hunger in the world, it is possible that the predicted food crisis of which the authors of *Famine-1975* and Cayce speak will be due to impending earth changes. As lands rise and sink around the globe, a lot of bread-baskets will be upset in the process! If the Great Lakes, for instance, are to empty into the Gulf of Mexico, this can only be by way of the Mississippi Valley. Thus will be lost an important food-producing region in this country. Other places for food raising will obviously have to be developed.

Casually, as was typical of the way such information came about, the possible answer for this future problem was volunteered. Bill Howard was told in 1944 that his birthplace—Livingston, Montana—was one day to be an important place. This city of the southern part of the state and its surroundings "will have much to do with many, many nations!" said his reading. He had been with Eric the Red in Minnesota, he was told, and had been one of those remaining there. He seems to have been drawn back to that area in this lifetime for a special purpose.

His reading went on to state, then, that "Saskatchewan, the Pampas area of the Argentine . . . portions of South Africa . . . these rich areas, with some portions of Montana and Nevada, must feed the world!"

There seems to be a tie-in between the two prophecies for Montana, particularly since they were given in the same reading. Livingston is not in the wheat-growing region of Montana but in the foothills of the Rockies. Could Cayce have meant that Livingston would become a food distribution center for the nations? This appears likely.

Saskatchewan in Canada adjoins Montana, making that part of the state likely to be most important as a source of food, as it is now. From the mention of the Pampas in the Argentine and parts of South Africa and Nevada, we have a clue as to what other lands might be relatively undisturbed by earth changes, if this is what the reading is referring to.

The trend has been away from the farms, for the little farmer, leaving food producing to the big business it has become. But has this been the best for our people, altogether? A Negro leader in October, 1967, might have set a new trend when he appeared on television and told about a group of his people in the Brooklyn ghettos who were planning a mass exodus to a farming community where they could "live under the sun." They wanted to get away from

79

the ghetto slums and crime, where their children had no place but the streets to play. They would establish farms for themselves and their families, he said, and "toil by day, plan by night."

Is a return to the soil the answer to much of our social and economic trouble? Cayce said in a reading that it didn't hurt anyone to get his fingers in the dirt now and then and work with the soil! Perhaps for many people this will be the answer.

Rural poverty, particularly in the South, is the opposite of what Cayce meant by a return to the soil, however, and of seventeen million such poor, only two million are served by Federal food programs, according to recent reports. Millions more, however, are benefiting from the "war on poverty," a program which has brought about pre-school training in the Head Start Project, job training under the Job Corps program, Vista and the Youth Corps.

In Norfolk, as its school systems' Office of Special Projects takes stock of twenty months of educating slum children better, a project spokesman states, "It will be ten or fifteen years before we see if we've been successful or not."*

In Los Angeles, "Operation Bootstrap" is a community project which approaches the problems of interracial understanding with practical classes in work skills and sessions in learning to communicate. In cities throughout the country "cultural enrichment" measures are being taken to give youngsters in slum areas an opportunity to learn dramatics, painting, dancing, writing.

These are the right steps, but they are late. Edgar Cayce warned in 1938 that unless America remembered to apply in its economic and political life the idea that we are our brother's keeper, there would be a revolution.

On November 1, 1967, Senator John McClellan, Chairman of the Senate Permanent Investigations subcommittee, told the opening hearing on slum violence that the riots over the past three years are becoming a "tangible threat to the preservation of law and order and our national security."

The subcommittee has found that since 1965, 130 per-

*Quoted in the *Virginian Pilot*, November 8, 1967

sons were killed and 3,623 wounded in major racial disturbances in seventy-six cities across the nation. The survey included the first civil rights march in Selma, Alabama, where no sniping, looting, arson or vandalism occurred, and followed through to the violence of the nation's cities in the summer of 1957. The statistics included "7,985 cases of arson, 28,939 arrests, 5,434 convictions, and economic loss estimated at $504.2 million."

Chairman McClellan expressed fear that this will "sweep us swiftly down the road to chaos and anarchy." Immediate causes of ghetto rioting, and later causes of longstanding social problems such as unemployment, were to be sought. Senator Karl Mundt, the subcommittee's senior Republican, warned that there was no limit to conflagration which could sweep this country and said that the first order of business should be "to lay down more firmly the law of the land."

If Edgar Cayce were living today, he could say no more to us than what he said on June 24, 1938, regarding the course to be taken now. "Since the application of these truths or tenets [the ideals of brotherhood] as indicated becomes the basic needs for the peoples of every land in the present, to be sure it behooves those in America, then, to apply same in their dealings with the situations that exist respecting the political, the economic, and the general situations throughout the land.

"This at the first glance may appear to be an impractical thing; yet these are the conditions to be met:

"Every phase of human experience and human relationship must be taken into consideration, just as indicated from that given, that we are our brother's keeper.

"Then if those in position to give of their means, their wealth, their education, their position, do not take these things into consideration, there must be that leveling that will come.

"For unless these are considered, there must eventually become a revolution in this country—and there will be a dividing of the sections as one against another. For these are the leveling means and manners to which men resort when there is the plenty in some areas and a lack of sustenance in the life of others.

"These are the manners in which such things as crime,

riots, and every nature of disturbance arise—in that those who are in authority are not considering every level, every phase of human activity and human experience.

"We find these conditions have been in other lands centralized, localized into individual activities—as in Russia, Italy, Germany. The conditions that exist in Spain, in China, in Japan are what? The oppression of the producers by those for whom and to whom such power has come to be used as their opportunity for becoming their brother's keeper: and not as represented in some lands, the disregarding of the other's rights.

"Then those who are in power must know that they are their brother's keeper and give expression to that which has been indicated in 'Thou shalt love the Lord with all thy heart and mind and body, and thy neighbor as thyself.'

"This rule must be applied. It is true that in some of these factions in Russia this is an attempt, yet there are those who have applied and do apply same in not only the economic life but attempt to in the mental and spiritual life. And this brings or works hardships where it should not be. . . .

"True, in other lands, whether the Communism, the Fascism or the Nazi regime, there are missions to be filled, and these are opportunities. But when there becomes class or mass distinction between this or that group, this or that party, this or that faction, then it becomes . . . a class rather than 'thy neighbor as thyself.'

"For all stand as one before Him. For the Lord is not a respecter of persons, and these things *cannot* long exist.

"From the conditions in these other lands, then, America—the United States—must take warning.

"For to whom does the wealth belong? To whom do the possibilities of the land belong?

"Does it belong to those who have inherited it? To those who have been given the position by power? Or to those who have, by their labor, by the sweat of their brow, produced same?

"Not that all would be had in common, as in the communistic idea, save as to keep that balance, to keep that oneness, to keep that association of ideas of activity, of the influences throughout the experiences of all. These are to be kept in those attunements which there may be the land, itself, defining what freedom is; in that each soul is by his own activity to be given the opportunity of expression, of labor, of producing.

"But all of these, also, are not to say where or what, but are to seek through their own ability, their own activity, to give that of themselves that is in keeping with those who labor in the vineyard of the Lord.

"Hence these may apply in the national and international relationships.

"For there must come, first, a stabilization of the monetary unit. There must come then the exchange of commodities of trade in a way and manner in which not merely sections, not merely distinctions made of one portion of the land against another, but all are taken into consideration.

"Unless this is done, turmoils and strifes will arise. And that which has made and does make the people of America afraid is the fear of servitude in any manner!

"All, though, must learn that those who are to be the greater, those who would make the greater contribution to activity in every sphere and phase of influence, are to be the servants of all; not those who would be lords over others. . . ."

On June 16, 1939, a questioner asked: "What should be our attitude toward the Negro and how may we best work out the karma created in relations with him?"

"He is thy brother!" Cayce reminded this person. "They that produced, they that brought servitude without thought or purpose, have created that which they must meet within their own principles, their own selves.

"These should be taken in the attitude of their own individual fitness, as in every other form of associations. For He hath made of one blood the nations of the earth."

"Is there a racial or social problem facing America?" asked one person.

"As indicated, these all depend upon the effort of individuals to all live as brothers one with another!" was the reply.

"How can it be met for the protection of our democracy?"

"Raise not democracy nor any other name above the brotherhood of man, the fatherhood of God!" Cayce reproved him.

"Since we are fighting for the freedom of all races," asked another person on June 20, 1943, "what suggestions could you give us toward effecting greater equality of opportunity for minority groups in our own country?"

"As indicated, in the first [reading on this subject], all groups must have their representation and their privileges, that they, too, may have the opportunity. Unless we begin within ourselves and our own household, we are false to ourselves and to the principles that we attempt to declare. By setting classes or masses against other groups, this is not brotherly love. . . ."

But the most final and ringing statement was given earlier than these, in 1938: "Though there may come those periods when there will be great stress, as brother rises against brother, as group or sect or race rises against race—yet the leveling must come.

"And only those who have set their ideal in Him and practiced it in their dealings with their fellowman may expect to survive the wrath of the Lord. . . .

"And then there should be, there will be, those rising to power that are able to meet the needs. For none are in power but that have been given the opportunity by the will of the Father—from which all power emanates.

"Hence, these will be leveled with the purpose 'My Word shall not fail!' "

VII

DESTINY OF NATIONS

The peace of the world will be shaped upon the American ideals and those found in the Masonic Order! "Not that the world is to become a Masonic Order," Cayce explained, but that the *ideals* will prevail.

The remarkable series of twenty-nine readings on world affairs—on peace, on world economics, race relations, and on America's place in the world—were given from 1921 to 1944. They became increasingly important as the world seemed to be getting into deeper waters. First the Depression, then World War II forced Cayce's friends to dig deeply for answers.

The destiny of nations is concerned with man's collective relationships with himself and with God. We can make of the world what we will—and we have! Future wars can be prevented by man's will, just as they are started that way. All evils begin in the hearts of men, and there they can be resolved. Cabot Lodge, on the televised program "Face the Nation" (September 17, 1967), stated that if the United Nations wanted to, it could mobilize member nations to thwart Communist aggression in Vietnam—*if* they had the will to do so!

In the readings on world problems are both prophecy for the latter part of this century, and counsel that is just as applicable now as when it was given. It is counsel that pulls no punches, for "God is not a respecter of persons." America has her faults, just as do other nations, and criticism of her was not withheld. Russia's religious development is to be the "hope of the world" one day, and China will be the "cradle of Christianity," although the implication is that the latter will not happen for a long time yet.

The gloomy picture we have of an earth changed and broken by natural disturbances is offset then by a much brighter picture of a world that *is* getting better, that is moving toward peace and order, in spite of the chaotic conditions in some respects. Cayce told us to measure whether or not the world was getting better by the same criterion which Christ used when He affirmed His Christhood—"Tell them the blind see, the lame walk." It is this kind of proof which we will see in the future, in fact, even now—and unless mankind is benefited in a real and practical way, we are deluding ourselves. He who tells a person who is starving, or without adequate housing, or without a job or self-respect, "Go in peace," is a "thief and a liar," said Cayce.

It is significant that he lived out his most effective years of service in Virginia, within a few miles from the place where a few Englishmen first set foot on these shores to begin there a new nation! It was in March, 1938, when many nations were about to be plunged into war, that he pointed out: "Each nation, each people have builded—by the very spirit of the peoples themselves—a purposeful position in the skein, the affairs, not only of the earth, but of the universe!"

In February, 1932, he was asked: "Please forecast the principal events for the next fifty years affecting the welfare of the human race."

"This had best be cast after the great catastrophe that's coming to the world in '36, in the form of the breaking up of many powers that now exist as factors in the world affairs. The first *noticeable* change will be the acceptance or rejection of the world's interference of Court of Last Resort in the world, in the present meeting as presented by France, and as rejected by America. Then with the breaking up in '36 will be the changes that will make different maps of the world."

"Name the powers that will be broken up in '36."

"Rather by '36. Will be Russia, U.S., Japan, and England or United Kingdom."

"Who will be the controlling power?"

"That depends upon who is closer to those sources of power."

In going back to the time of this reading, history has recorded a decade of shaken world powers, during which 1936 was a particularly violent and fateful year. Leading up to those years was Hitler's rise to power in 1933, and Germany's withdrawal from the League of Nations.

But in 1936 we find these events:

In England, George V died in January and Edward abdicated in December, causing his brother, the Duke of York, to become King George VI.

Spain began civil war.

Russia's Stalin started conducting his Great Purge Trials (half a million people executed, imprisoned, or put into forced labor camps).

Italy and Germany formed the Rome-Berlin axis in October.

Hitler denounced the Locarno Treaty and marched into the Rhineland.

By the end of the year, almost all nations had abandoned the gold standard.

In 1938, Spain was presented as a trouble spot for the rest of the globe. "This is that whereunto the real troubles, here, are only beginning," stated a reading. "For unless there is to be the consideration given to each factor, then others will come in and devour the spoils.

"This is the outcome of seed sown in the ages past, and from same man can—as a whole—and should—take warning."

Spain's war was the preamble to World War II when German Nazis, Italian Fascists, and Russian Communists took sides by sending troops, supplies, and technicians.

On January 15, 1932, Cayce was asked: "Will Italy adopt a more liberal form of government in the near future?"

"Rather that of a more monarchical government than that of the liberal," Cayce replied. "Italy, too, will be broken by what now is an insignificant or small power that lies between those of the other larger, or those of the moment, of the larger. These will not come, as we find . . . before the catastrophes of outside forces to the earth in

'36, which will come from the shifting of the equilibrium of the earth itself in space, with those of the consequential effects upon the various portions of the country—or world—affected by same."

Italy met defeat in Greece and in North Africa in 1940.

On June 13, 1939, Cayce stated, "Then ye ask, What is to be the outcome of England and France in their efforts to join hands with Russia as an encirclement of the totalitarian regime? These, so long as they are in keeping with God's purposes with man, will succeed. When they become active for self-preservation without thought or purpose of their fellowman, they must fail.

"So it is with the endeavors of Germany, Italy, Japan. As they attempt to preserve their own personalities, their own selves without thought of their fellowman, they may succeed for the moment, but 'God is not mocked!' And whatsoever a man, a country, a nation sows, that it must reap."

In 1932 when Great Britian was trying to cope with the "non-cooperation" of Gandhi in India's civil disobedience campaigns, the World Affairs series answered this question: "From the general trend of events, what is to be expected in the struggle between Great Britain and India?"

"Great Britian is *losing* an excellent fight. Non-resistance is hard to be broken! As to whether those peoples will remain or whether the prayers and supplications of others will be with those, depends upon individuals."

A year later, Cayce was asked: "Give the outstanding events which may be expected in the struggle between Great Britain and India."

"Those that have already come to pass, in the things that have just happened, in the recognition of the low caste and the outcasts, or the untouchables. And this *has* been accomplished and will go farther."

England was described in the readings as the "balancing power" in the world. When England begins to consider every phase of her relationships with other countries, "more and more will it be able to control the world for peace."

"The spirit of France will not be broken," Cayce predicted on January 21, 1944. That was a dark time, indeed. France had been occupied by Germany since 1942 and it was to be five months before her liberation by the Allies.

States another reading: "There is that which is the spirit

**EDGAR CAYCE FOUNDATION and
A.R.E. LIBRARY/CONFERENCE CENTER**
Virginia Beach, Va.

OVER 50 YEARS OF SERVICE

NO POSTAGE
NECESSARY
IF MAILED
IN THE
UNITED STATES

BUSINESS REPLY CARD
First Class Permit No. 2456, Virginia Beach, Va.

POSTAGE WILL BE PAID BY

A.R.E.®
P.O. Box 595
Virginia Beach, VA 23451

785-71

of France. Don't ever get the idea that even under the stress through which the nation of France is passing, it will be eliminated from the earth. It is as one of the seven sins, as well as one of the twelve virtues in the human family."

He described the French situation then as "an old debt that must eventually be paid."

So nations, like people, have karma and must pay for past crimes against brother nations!

China

A book publisher in August, 1943, planned to visit China on a mission "for improving the future of cultural relations as they affect books between this country and China in the years after the war." He asked Edgar Cayce for advice for making his mission a success.

Cayce began: "As will be seen, the greater rule in the next twenty-five years in China is to grow towards the Christian faith (though it may appear to some at present that this is lacking). . . ."

Would China's leadership take a more democratic or more authoritarian turn in the next twenty-five years?

"More of the democratic" was the answer. "For, as has been indicated, more and more will those of the Christian faith come to be in political positions, and this in China will mean the greater rule in certain groups—according to how well they manifest. And these will progress, for civilization moves west.

"The various sects of China (Christian, Buddhist, Confucian?) will all be united more and more towards the democratic way—just as it has begun and as it has been in the last twenty years, and it will grow and spread faster in the next twenty-five, and more in the last five, than in the first ten."

For a prediction to be so explicit and emphatic, this one would appear twenty-five years after to be dead wrong. Those years—1923 to 1968—have seen a distressing turn, not toward Christian leadership, or a free democracy, but toward a ruthless dictatorship under Communism.

It is true that China had already taken a step towards democracy in 1911 when she revolted against the ineffectual Manchu dynasty. The Nationalist Party ruled beginning in 1928 and represented a people's government which made quite a contrast against the emperors of the past. But Chiang Kai-shek's forces were defeated in 1949 and a new government, the People's Republic of China, was set up. Millions of Christians and people of other faiths, and other intellectuals, were now killed off or "re-educated" in Mao's purges.

Could prayer have saved China from this? "If the same attitude (of prayer) is kept in China," Cayce told another person about that time, "the eventual conquering of self in China will be brought about and there will be lack of interference then from without."

There had already been "interference from without" for years in China. In 1938, Edgar Cayce was asked about the "Japanese and Chinese situation," referring to Japan's undeclared, all-out war on China beginning the year before. "These bespeak of themselves that which is happening and has happened," was the reply. "But might does not make right. Rather will the principles of the Christian faith be carried forward in and through the turmoils that are a part of both China and Japan. For without those cleansings and purifyings, tradition (of feudalism) alone may not be destroyed. For it is through the purging that the strength and the beauty of each will come forth."

The purging by war, by Mao, and by civil war—the last of which still goes on—is what Cayce meant, we think. That any religious life can still survive the watchful and ever present eye of the present government is almost too much to hope. Yet, that is what Cayce seems to say, and what is more, the principles of Christian faith will be carried forward "in and through" these turmoils.

But there are other predictions he made which tell the present picture quite accurately, if we interpret them aright. In 1932, he declared: "The international interference will make for a repeopling of portions of China, and the ultimate destruction of China or Japan as a nation!"

It appears that he meant the time of wars between China and powerful nations including Great Britian, Japan, and France at the turn of the century. The victors in each war, in which China was consistently defeated, took over much of her territory, "leased" her ports, maintained troops on her soil. It was this desperate and humiliating situation that led the Chinese to overthrow the Manchus and reform their government. Under Mao, many people have been transported from the east to the western lands to develop towns, industries, and agriculture. Is this what Edgar Cayce meant by "a repeopling of portions of China?"

The last part of this prediction sees "the ultimate destruction of China or Japan as a nation!" This was, as we interpret it, to be an outcome of the "international interference" spoken of in the first part of the prophecy. If a nation consists in its traditions, its religions, its arts, the philosophy which gives it the indefinable character distinguishing it from other nations, then the old China has been destroyed as a nation. In Mao's "cultural revolution," the young men of his Red Guard have recently led in an unbelievably savage rampage to tear down and to demolish every vestige of the symbols of China's past. Temples and their ancient treasures have been burned, along with books and religious statues. Poetry inscribed on mountain rock among the temples in Central China has been obliterated (*Life*, October 7, 1966).

The American book publisher in that far-off day in 1943—when the temples still stood, and one could talk about an interchange of ideas between the United States and China—was told by Cayce that he should cultivate the intelligentsia. The most helpful would be the Christians and those Chinese who had been educated in America. He was told also that an exchange of books between the two countries should be accompanied by stressing ideas upon which both could agree. He was advised to avoid getting side-tracked into one sect or group.

In our continuing attempt to understand China in the light of the Edgar Cayce prophecies, we might turn to *The Nature and Truth of the Great Religions* by Dr. A. K. Reischauer (Charles E. Tuttle, 1966) which states: "for more than a century now the Chinese have come more and more into contact with the Western world and a civilization enriched by what modern science can provide for a good and better life. As a result of this China is seen now by many Chinese themselves as a backward country and it is perhaps only natural that some of them should blame especially Confucianism just because of its traditional glorification of the past. . . .

91

"Sooner or later even those who are now so favorably impressed with the Communist program of doing something positive about their country's backwardness and improving its economic conditions, will realize that man, just because he is man, 'does not live by bread alone.' Whether that means that the Chinese people will then turn again to Confucianism and their other age-old spiritual heritage remains to be seen. That there is much in the best of this heritage that is of permanent value cannot be questioned by any fair-minded student. It is, however, quite likely that this heritage will be reinterpreted and modified by the influence of the Western world's spiritual heritage and so bring it more in line with what might be called our developing common World culture. . . ."

Russia

Echoing Dr. Reischauer's above statement, the title of a recent book by novelist Vladimir Dudintsev about the "dreariness and stagnation of Russian life"* is *Not By Bread Alone.*

In 1932, Cayce prophesied that "on Russia's religious development will come the greater hope of the world." He gave a cosmic picture of what had happened to Russia in the years of revolt against the Czar and he described that country as "being born again." He defined America's relationship to Europe with the words: "the hope of Europe depends upon *you,* in your homes *today!"*

That thought was brought into sharp focus recently when Svetlana Alliluyeva, Stalin's daughter, appealed to the free world to speak out for freedom everywhere.

Cayce was asked, "What can be expected in the trends of events in the political and economic conditions in Europe?"

"Europe is as a house broken up," was the answer. "Some years ago there was the experience of a mighty peoples being overridden for the gratification and satisfaction of a few, irrespective of any other man's right. That peoples are going through the experience of being born again and is the thorn in the flesh to many a political and fi-

*Robert Sherrod, "Russia at the Crossroads," *Post,* March 26, 1966.

nancial nation in Europe, in the world. But out of same, with the prayers and supplications of those that may pray—even as Abram or Abraham, 'If there be fifty, will it not be spared? O, if there be ten faithful, will it not be spared?' Then, the hope of Europe depends upon *you,* in your own home *today!* In not the same way, but the same manner as did the life of Lot, or of the other peoples in Sodom and Gomorrah."

"What is the name of that nation referred to?"

"Russia!"

This was, of course, pointing to the sufferings of the Russians under the Czarist regime, and the overthrow of that regime in 1917. We might remind ourselves that Stalin's purges had not yet taken place, nor had Hitler risen to power, at the time of this reading. Cayce seemed to be urging Americans to pray for Europe to spare it the fate similar to that of the biblical Sodom and Gomorrah.

Five years later, in 1938, Europe was suffering that fate, and now Cayce said of Russia that "a new understanding has and will come to a troubled people. Here, because of the yoke of oppression, because of the self-indulgences, has arisen another extreme. Only when there is freedom of speech, the right to worship according to the dictates of the conscience—until these come about, still turmoils will be within." This time, it was not the Czar's Russia of which he spoke, but that of Stalin.

Cayce foresaw the changes that have come about economically between the two countries. When he was asked in 1933 if the United states should recognize the Soviet government, he said: "Many conditions should be considered, were this to be answered correctly. You could say yes and no, and both be right, with the present attitude of both peoples as a nation, and both be wrong, for there *is* to come, there *will* come, an entire change in the attitude of both nations as powers in the financial and the economic world. As for those raw resources, Russia surpasses all other nations. As for abilities to development of same, those in the U.S. are the farthest ahead. Then these united or upon an equitable basis, would become or could become, powers (for good); but there are many interferences for those . . . investments (already made), those already under questions; (these) will take years to settle."

Recently, Russia has become increasingly capitalistic in her economics, according to reports. The U.S. has, we see, turned from isolationsim since 1938 to a policy of world-wide involvement in the financial and economic welfare of other nations.

As for the prediction that her religious development will be the basis for the "hope of the world," we are reminded by experts on Russia who have lived and traveled in that country that her Russian Orthodox Church has never been entirely eliminated from the life of the people. To some extent, marriages, baptisms, Easter and Christmas celebrations continue to take place in the ancient churches. The experts further tell us that the ideal of brotherhood and the community working together for the common good is also a part of the Russian heritage, which perhaps explains the emphasis they have accepted, in the extreme, on the collective society, at the expense of the individual.

This is not to obscure the facts that children are taught atheism from the cradle onward, with "no other principles than what the Party teaches," that all religions are scorned; and that church leadership is kept subjugated and ineffectual for the general masses.*

But out of extremity often develops the opposite extreme, and within the past ten years, a stirring has been felt among the religious and intellectual elements in Russia, an evidence of desire to break the bonds that hold mind and spirit. In the 1950's, Boris Pasternak's *Dr. Zhivago* spoke for the "other Russia." In reporting the effect of this novel, Eugene Lyons stated that "there is more than a chance that the outlawed novel will do its destined work of spiritual mobilization."** More than five hundred copies of the book in its original Russian have circulated in that country, according to Lyons, and we assume they continue to do so.

Another hero, in Western eyes, is the late Oleg Penkovskiy, key member of the Soviet intelligence service, who was shot in Moscow in 1963 for passing top-secret documents to the west for a period of sixteen months. Ac-

---

The Penkovskiy Papers (New York: Doubleday, 1965).
**The Book the Kremlin is Afraid to Let the Russians Read," *Reader's Digest,* February, 1959. Used with permission.

cording to the editors of a book telling his views on Russia, *The Penkovskiy Papers* (Doubleday and Co., 1965): "Experts assess Penkovskiy's achievement as the greatest intelligence *coup* of modern times. Singlehandedly he sabotaged Kruschev's threatened Berlin showdown in 1961 and his information lay behind President Kennedy's successful defeat of the Soviet Cuban missile threat in October, 1962."

His friend Greville Wynne, a British spy who was his go-between, described Penkovskiy as being "interested in religion. He had indeed been baptized himself by his pious mother. . . ." And further: "He believed simply that a free society should emerge in the Soviet Union, and that it could only come by toppling the only government he knew. He was a heroic figure."

Incidents such as this one, and others which have been recounted in the press, seem to point to a growing movement in Russia toward freedom of religion and expression, and while they do not do more than provide a hopeful glimmer, they could be the beginnings of the "religious development" which Edgar Cayce said would one day prove to be the "hope of the world."

Further evidence for this trend is presented in the account of still another observer, James H. Billington, who spent seven months in Russia in 1966.

In the November 10, 1967, issue of *Life* Magazine, Billington wrote: "Svetlana Stalin is not alone in rejecting the faith of her parents for that of her grandparents. Repelled by both the manipulative morality and monotonous art of the Stalinist bureaucracy, young Russians now seek a deeper basis for human conduct and esthetic inspiration. 'Faith proved itself worthy of fresh respect in the camps,' one survivor of more than a decade of imprisonment told me. 'Those who believed in God often seemed the only ones able to go on acting like men.' But the intellectuals are not seeking mere return to the Orthodox Church of yore. 'Even if I were free to do so, I could never join a church which did not even pray publicly for those in the camps during the Stalin era,' one writer explained."

Mr. Billington goes on to say that "the Russian intelligentsia has a kind of undoctrinal ecumenical movement of its own; it brings together Christians and Jews (far closer in Russia, where they share a common persecution, than in the West, where they share an occasional brotherhood banquet table), neo-Kantian scientists, pro-Buddhist Orientalists, and many other forms of believers. All identify vaguely with Russia's religious past; and many feel attracted to new sects or religious-philosophical discussion groups, where they hope to find more satisfying human association than in the philistine society about them. Youthful members of such a religious-philosophical group were apparently victimized by the wave of quiet arrests conducted in Leningrad early in 1967. . . ."

Edgar Cayce's suggestion that Americans and Russians might learn to cooperate in solving the world's supply problems is brought to mind by Mr. Billington's proposal that "new bi-national Russo-American scientific and cultural projects might start us on the path toward new practical forms of collaboration that should help bypass old hostilities. Such projects (preferably under auspices of the U.N.) would never seek to exclude others, and should begin with projects of common concern to all humanity."

"What Then of Nations?"

In the last World Affairs reading, given June 22, 1944, Edgar Cayce said that spiritual laws govern the actions of nations as much as those of individuals. He had, as we pointed out earlier, said that nations had their characters, and that by their choices and actions they created their places not only in the world, but in the universe, as well.

Cayce explained how the nations became separated by languages or "tongues," when they "set about to seek their gratifications." "There are then in the hearts, the minds, of men, various concepts of these [spiritual] laws and as to where and to what they are applicable. . . ."

It was in misapplying God's laws that the nations have suffered, he said. "What is the spirit of America?" he challenged. "Most individuals proudly boast 'freedom.' Freedom of what? When ye bind men's hearts and minds through various ways and manners, does it give them freedom of speech? Freedom of worship? Freedom from want?

Not unless these basic principles are applicable, for God meant man to be free. . . .

"What then of nations? In Russia there comes the hope of the world, not as that sometimes termed of the communistic, of the Bolshevik, no; but freedom, freedom! That each man will live for his fellow man! The principle has been born. It will take years for it to be crystallized, but out of Russia comes again the hope of the world. Guided by what? That friendship with the nation that hath even set on its present monetary unit 'In God We Trust.' (Do ye use that in thine own heart when you pay your just debts? Do ye use that in thy prayer when ye send thy missionaries to other lands? 'I give it, for in God we trust'? Not for the other fifty cents, either!)

"In the application of these principles, in those forms and manners in which the nations of the earth have and do measure to those in their activities, yea, to be sure, America may boast; but rather is that principle being forgotten when such is the case, and that is the sin of America.

"So in England, from whence have come the ideas—not the ideals—ideas of being just a little bit better than the other fellow. Ye must *grow* to that in which ye will deserve to be known, deserve to receive. That has been, that is, the sin of England.

"As in France, to which this principle first appealed, to which then came that which was the gratifying of the desires of the body—that is the sin of France.

"In that nation which was first Rome, when there was that unfolding of those [Christian] principles, its rise, its fall, what were they that caused the fall? The same as at Babel. The dissensions, the activities that would enforce upon these, in this or that sphere, servitude, that a few might just agree, that a few even might declare their oneness with the Higher forces. For theirs was the way that seemeth right to a man but the end is death. That is the sin of Italy.

"The sin of China? Yea, there is the quietude that will not be turned aside, saving itself by the slow growth. There has been a growth, a stream through the land in ages which asks to be left alone to be just satisfied with that within itself. It awoke one day and cut its hair off! This, here, will be one day the cradle of Christianity, as applied in the lives of men. Yea, it is far off as man counts time, but only a day in the heart of God—for tomorrow China will awake. Let each and every soul as they come to their understandings, do something, then, in his or her own heart.

"Just as in India, the cradle of knowledge not applied, except within self. What is the sin of India? Self, and left the 'ish' off—just self!"

Israel

Edgar Cayce said that human affairs move in cycles. Concerning Palestine, God apparently worked in cycles of milleniums. In studying the biblical prophecies and those of Cayce we arrive at a better understanding of prophecy in general, and that concerning Israel, in particular.

The Israelites first moved into Palestine about 2,000 B.C. according to history. Egyptian texts mention Jerusalem about 1,900 B.C. A thousand years later, King David set up there the Ark of the Covenant. After another thousand years, Jesus of Nazareth was born in Bethlehem and the Temple which had been destroyed by the Romans was rebuilt by Herod the Great. Approximately a thousand years after the Jews left Palestine in 70 A.D., the Turks captured Jerusalem. It remained under Moslem rule until freed during World War I, 1917, and under the British mandate the World Zionist Movement to bring the Jews back to their homeland began. But it will be 2,072 before the cycle is completed.

In 1933, fifteen years before the Jews proclaimed the state of Israel, Edgar Cayce foretold that, as it had been prophesied in the Bible, the Jews would return. This came about in questions on the part of some who were then concerned about Hitler's attitude toward the Jews.

When this reading was given (November 4, 1933) Hitler had just come into power and as Cayce has stated elsewhere, "even God does not know what man will do." Cayce could not at that point foretell what course Hitler would take.

He termed the events then happening and consequent

events involving the Jews' return to Palestine "the beginning of the return that must come throughout the earth."

How timely are the biblical prophecies for the Jews of the 1960's! Palestine was, under the British, divided for fifty years into Arab and Jewish nations. By June, 1967, in the "Seventy-two-hour War," they fulfilled the final prophecies concerning their long struggle with the Arabs and their other traditional enemies:

"Thus says the Lord God: Behold, I will take the people of Israel from the nations among which they have gone, and will gather them from all sides, and bring them to their own land; and I will make them one nation in the land, upon the mountains of Israel; and one king shall be king over them all; and they shall be no longer two nations, and no longer divided into two kingdoms." (Ezekiel 37:21-23)

We think of the amazing development since 1948 of Palestine from an arid land and swamp to the garden place it is now becoming. The Jews have answered a call home from far places, a call that is two thousand years old.

A special insight into the restoration of Israel is given in the Cayce readings which see the Jews and their long history of wandering as the dramatization of all of man's spiritual condition, and not just that of one small nation. Israel, said Cayce, is all those on earth who are seeking a way back to God. Thus, we share vicariously with the Jews their heritage, their traditions of oneness with God, their falling away from him, their trials. "Israel" means the spiritual seekers of the world, no matter if Buddhist, Christian, American, French, German, or "Hottentot," as Cayce said it.

The Bible itself brings all of us into the picture in predicting that there would be no more wars, which Cayce emphasized was coming about for us in this century:

For out of Zion shall go forth the law,
    and the word of the Lord from Jerusalem.
He shall judge between many peoples,
    and shall decide for strong nations afar off;
and they shall beat their swords into plowshares,
    and their spears into pruning hooks;
nation shall not lift up sword against nation,

neither shall they learn war anymore;
but they shall sit every man under his vine and under his
  fig tree, and none shall make them afraid;
for the mouth of the Lord of hosts has spoken. (Micah
4:2-4)

A particularly inscrutable prediction was given in 1941 for a two-year-old boy that he would live to see a "religious war." So far, this is one problem the world hasn't had to face, unless it could be the Israeli-Arab conflict which still goes unresolved.

VIII

"FOR THE SEEKER TO KNOW"

In the desert near Cairo the pyramid ruins extend for sixty miles west of the Nile River. The one nearest the Nile is the oldest, the Great Pyramid of Gizeh, called by Cayce the "Pyramid of Understanding." It is the largest of them all, standing 481 feet high. Between this and the Nile is the Sphinx, facing east.

The Great Pyramid is conjectured to have been built around 2885 B.C. The Egyptian King Khufu built it as a tomb, say historians, after a mere century and a quarter of progress from the time stone masonry was first used. Suddenly, Egypt leaped in architectural prowess for constructing primitive pit graves to the most advanced building ever known. Clearly, there is something wrong with our understanding about the culture that produced it!

Much has been written about the mysterious Pyramid and its guardian Sphinx. Studies by mathematicians, historians, and architects reveal it to be a puzzle in stone, based on mathematical, geometric proportions.

According to Dr. Browne Landone, author of "The Prophecies in the Ancient Temples,"* the mathematics involved in the Pyramid of Gizeh is the Teleois, "a mysterious series of numbers and proportions found . . . in musical scales, distances of planets from the sun, designs in snowflakes, et cetera. It also determines the structures of all key temples of Palestine and Tibet, ancient Cathay, Mayaland and the eastern Andes. . . . In the structure of

*in Gordon Collier's *Will You Be Alive in 1975?* (Tarrytown, N. Y.: The Book of Destiny. 1961).

the Pyramid of Gizeh the Teleois is so dominant that we are forced to believe that it was intentionally used to symbolize and record knowledge of the past and prophecies of the future. . . ."

Out of the hundreds of references to what are called in the Edgar Cayce data the "Pyramid Prophecies," or "Egypt, Prehistory," comes a story that, if true, is of the greatest importance to our understanding of both the past and the future. In the story of Atlantis and the earth changes that continent suffered, we have the background for Cayce's prophecies dealing with the Great Pyramid Mystery.

The ending of Atlantis was roughly the beginning of Egypt, and other cultures. One of the major ideas to come out of the Cayce data is that the time of the construction of the Great Pyramid was not 2,885 B.C., as is suggested by James Henry Breasted in *Ancient Times* (Boston: Ginn and Co., 1935) but 10,490 to 10,390 B.C.!

Scholars are bemused by the unbelievably rapid technological and scientific progress which the Egyptians are supposed to have made in little more than a century, in building the Pyramid. That they must have developed such a sophisticated concept of architecture under the leadership of a more advanced people seems more plausible than that they achieved these highly complicated arts suddenly, by themselves.

According to Edgar Cayce, just such a culture emerged from the ingress of hordes of Atlantean refugees into Egypt 12,500 years ago. Egypt was one of the safety lands during the destruction of the Lemurian and Atlantean civilizations. These destructions occurred, Cayce said, over long periods of time: The break-up of Atlantis took place over a period of 7,500 years, between 15,650 and 8,150 B.C.

By dint of their superiority over the native Egyptians, the Atlanteans conquered the latter and imposed upon them their religion and civilization. A peaceful settlement was brought about by Atlanteans and Egyptians but there were many races and nations now existing here and therefore a conglomerate of ideas and influences.

Egypt was thought by the Atlanteans to be the ideal place in which to establish not only a high culture, but a new spiritual understanding. This was due to the persistent influence of the "children of the Law of One," or the religious element. There grew up an exchange of ideas with people of other lands such as the "Poseidian (or remnants of Atlantis) Og, Norway, China, India, Peru and America." At that time, there was also one common language. The Atlantean leaders made visits to these other lands to study and collect spiritual ideas from other centers.

Egypt became a "land of plenty" in "foods, in ornaments, in the recreation, in the needs of the inner man, in the many material things of life, and in the development of the sciences." The land was visited by the "wise men" of other countries now, which was in reciprocation to Atlantean visits. A wise government was established, evolving a "national spirit and centralization of interests."

The leaders of this new nation had the task of teaching spiritual laws that "there might be a closer relationship of man to the Creator and of man to man." This was the thesis of their mission, which they felt inspired by God to carry out.

In special temples they prepared the records of Atlantis from its beginnings and "those things that were to make known later in the minds of peoples as the changes came about in the earth." The Great Pyramid, however, was the final statement. Begun in 10,490 B.C., it was to take one hundred years to build. "The rise and fall of the nations were to be depicted in this same temple that was to act as an interpreter for that which had been, that which is, and that which is to be, in the material plane." It would record further "all changes in the religious thought of the world."

It was in the Hall of Records, however, that actual written documents were put which would explain in full the message of the Great Pyramid.

Concerning the magnificent achievement in establishing the records in stone and in written hieroglyphics, Cayce raised the question as to why this would be accomplished in Egypt, rather than some other place. "Why Egypt? This had been determined . . . as the center of the universal activities of nature, as well as the spiritual forces, and where there might be the least disturbance by the convulsive movements which came about in the earth through the destruction of Lemuria, Atlantis, and—in later periods— the flood . . .

"When the lines about the earth are considered from the mathematical precisions, it will be found that the center is nigh unto where the Great Pyramid, which was begun then, is still located.

"Then, there were the mathematical, the astrological, and the numerological indications, as well as the indiviual urge. . . ."

One person was told by Edgar Cayce that he had helped to build the Sphinx!

"In what capacity did this entity act regarding the building of the Sphinx?" he asked.

"As the monuments were being rebuilt in the plains of that now called the Pyramid of Gizeh, this entity builded, laid, the foundations; that is, superintended same, figured out the geometrical position of same as [in] relation to those buildings as were put up of that connecting the Sphinx, and the data concerning same may be found in the vaults in the base of the Sphinx. The entity was with that dynasty . . . when these buildings [were] begun. This laid out, base of Sphinx, in channels, and in the corner facing the Gizeh may be found that of the wording of how this was founded, giving the history . . ."

Information regarding the Sphinx "and many findings, as given, may be found in the base of the left forearm, or leg, of the prostrate beast, in the base of foundation. Not in the underground channel (as was opened by the ruler many years, many centuries, later) but in the real base, or that as would be termed in the present parlance as the cornerstone. . . ."

The Hall of Records

Scores of allusions are made to the future opening of the Hall of Records "when much may be brought to light." Located in a small tomb or pyramid of its own, according to Cayce, it lies between the right paw of the Sphinx and the Nile River and is a kind of "time capsule." Cayce calls it "the pyramid of unknown origin, as yet"—a "storehouse of records"—"that holy mount yet not uncovered."

These, first, include the "precious" records of Atlantis put there by one who was in charge of the records when the last of the Atlanteans scattered. A good number of others brought records with them, as well. These documents, described as "copies" of the Atlantean originals, included their scientific knowledge, their literature, history, laws, and treatises on "the abilities to use the unseen forces in the . . . material things of man."

Still other works were "for the interpreting of the earth as it was, as it is, and as it is to be" for the "seeker to know his relationships to the past, the present, and the future when counted from the material standpoint."

Such data is gleaned from readings like the following: "The entity was among those of the Atlanteans who came into Egypt and whose land was destroyed during that period. Hence, the entity was among the Children of the Law of One that entered the Egyptian land, being a priestess of Poseidia, and brought much of the record that was attempted to be preserved for future activity, future proofs of those who would seek out those influences that were the happenings in the Atlantean land. . . ."

Another reading, for one of the builders who laid out the plans for these tombs, speaks not of only one Record Chamber, but of "many."

According to Cayce, the people who had gathered and compiled the sacred records were buried there in those tombs, along with many artifacts which will provide further meaningful evidence of the existence of this people. Among them are innumerable articles which had been deposited in the tombs as having particular significance to the persons buried there. These include musical instruments, such as harps, lyres, lutes, and even violas. There will be found "the hangings, the accoutrements for the altar in the temple of the day." Gold and precious stones, used for both healing and for exchange, are there. There will be uncovered "the cymbals for the calling of the people to worship"; plaques and life seals; surgical instruments and medical compounds.

A woman named Ammelle of Atlantis "persuaded her countrymen to preserve drawings, recipes, placards" and led in "the first attempt to make for a written language" in order to preserve the records in Egypt.

Another's "harps and menus" will be "in the storehouse of records."

In the Hall of Records, the linens one woman prepared

will be discovered. "Caskets of gold, or the golden bands about those [bodies were] put into the burial chambers."

In the "mount not yet uncovered" is buried the king, together with a number of his effects. At least one person for whom Cayce gave a reading was told that he, too, was buried there. Besides the many temples built around the Sphinx, mention is made of an area or city that is just beyond the Great Pyramid. "And many of the inner shrines will today, now, be found bearing the inscription of the entity in that period—Isssi—"

Of particular interest to scholars is that the records were put in forms that were "partially of the old characters of the ancient or early Egyptian and part in the newer form of the Atlanteans."

Here in this hidden chamber, then, is "a record of Atlantis from the beginnings of those periods when the Spirit took form or began the encasements in that land, and the developments of the peoples throughout their sojourn, with the record of the first destruction and the changes that took place in the land, with the record of the sojourning of the peoples to the varied activities in other lands, and a record of the meetings of all the nations or lands for the activities in the destructions that became necessary, with the final destruction of Atlantis and the buildings of the pyramid of initiation, with who, what, where, would come the opening of the records that are as copies from the sunken Atlantis; for with the change it must rise again."

"This in position lies, as the sun rises from the waters, the line of the shadow (or light) falls between the paws of the Sphinx, that was later set as the sentinel or guard, and which may not be entered from the connecting chambers from the Sphinx's paw (right paw) until the time has been fulfilled when the changes must be active in this sphere of man's experience. Between, then, the Sphinx and the river."

These records were made from the standpoint of world movements, and not merely from that of one nation, Cayce reminded one person. He said that it would be necessary to wait until the full time has come for the breaking up of much that has been in the nature of selfish motives in the world, before they could be obtained.

One woman was told that her tomb was a part of the

Hall of Records and that there were thirty-two plates or tablets there which "may be discovered by 1958." That date is now a decade past and so the world still waits. As for herself, this person was told she was so gifted intuitively that she might obtain the records mentally!

In the reading on the prophecies of the Great Pyramid, the question was asked, "Are the deductions and conclusions arrived at by D. Davidson and H. Aldersmith in their book on the Great Pyramid correct?"

"Many of these that have been taken as deductions are correct. Many are overdrawn. Only an initiate may understand," was the answer.

The volume is entitled *The Great Pyramid, Its Divine Message*. This classic, now out of print, was first published in 1924. Its final and seventh printing was in 1948. Just what parts are correct and what are overdrawn would indeed take an initiate to know, so that the reader must decide for himself what to take for his authority. There are many charts and diagrams of the Great Pyramid showing its perfect placement in relation to the Sphinx, the earth, and the universe, of which Cayce made mention. There are, however, many statements and a good deal of lore that match other sources, and the book is founded upon the day's best scholars of the antiquities, including Breasted.

Like Cayce, Davidson and Aldersmith describe a highly developed civilization in pre-dynastic Egypt. There was a catastrophe of worldwide proportions after which nothing tangible remained. Modern civilization was founded upon oral traditions brought over from former civilizations. The authors point out that in all the ancient cultures of Egypt, Mexico, Peru, Babylonia, Assyria, and China there are various versions of the Noachian Deluge.

They further state that "the day generally celebrated throughout the world in ancient and modern times as the Anniversary of the Catastrophe, is November 1, with variations generally from October 31 to November 2. These represent in modern times All Hallows' Eve, All Saints' Day, and All Souls' Day."

One particular statement stands out in bold-face: "The object of the Pyramid's Message was to proclaim Jesus as Deliverer and Saviour of men, to announce the dated circumstances relating to His Coming, and to prepare men by means of its Message—whether they believe it or not in the first instance—to adapt themselves spiritually to the circumstances of His coming when the fact of the Message becomes to them a matter of certainty."

This agrees with the Cayce interpretation, and, as we see it, is the key to all the rest. We leave to students a comparison of the contents of this book with what we present here from the Cayce record.

At 3 p.m. on June 30, 1932, members of the Norfolk Study Group One and friends of A.R.E. met to hear Edgar Cayce give his usual reading for the Annual Congress. References had been made many times to the Pyramid prophecies and now, details were to be requested as to the origin, purpose, and the prophecies, themselves. The reading was as follows:

"Yes. In the information as respecting the pyramids, their purpose in the experience of the peoples, in the period when there was the rebuilding of the priest during the return in the land, some 10,500 years before the coming of the Christ into the land, there was first that attempt to restore and add to that which had been begun on what is called the Sphinx, and the treasure or storehouse facing same, between this and the Nile, in which those records were kept. . . .

"Then . . . there began the building of that now called Gizeh, with which those prophecies that had been in the Temple of Records and the Temple Beautiful were builded, in the building of this that was to be the Hall of the Initiates. . . .

"This, then, receives all the records from the beginnings of that given by the priest . . . to the return of the Great Initiate to that and other lands for the folding up of those prophecies that are depicted there. All changes that came in the religious thought in the world are shown there, in the variations in which the passage through same is reached, from the base to the top—or to the open tomb and the top. These are signified by both the layer and the color in what direction the turn is made.

"This, then, is the purpose for the record and the meaning to be interpreted by those that have come and do come as the teachers of the various periods, in the experience of this present position, of the activity of the spheres, of the earth.

"In the period that is to come, this ends—as to that point which is between what is termed in chronological time in present—between 1950 and 1958, but there have been portions that have been removed by those that desecrated many of those other records in the same land. This was rejected by that Pharaoh who hindered in the peoples' leaving the land.

"Q. 1. Are the deductions and conclusions arrived at by D. Davidson and H. Aldersmith in their book on the Great Pyramid correct?

"A. 1. Many of these that have been taken as deductions are correct. Many are overdrawn. Only an initiate may understand.

"Q. 2. What corrections for the period of the twentieth century?

"A. 2. Only those that there will be an upheaval in '36.

"Q. 3. Do you mean there will be an upheaval in '36 as recorded in the Pyramid?

"A. 3. As recorded in the Pyramid, though this is set for a correction which, as has been given, is between '32 *and* '38—the correction would be, for this—as seen—is '36—for it is in many—these run from specific days; for, as has been seen, there are periods when even the hour, day, year, place, country, nation, town, and individuals are pointed out. That's how correct are many of those prophecies as made.

"Oft may there be changes that bring periods, as seen in that period when there was an alteration in that initiate in the land of Zu and Ra that *brought* a change, but at a different point because of being driven by those that were set as the guides or guards of same.

"In this same pyramid did the Great Initiate, the Master, take those last of the Brotherhood degrees with John, the forerunner of Him, at that place. As is indicated in that period where the entrance is shown to be in that land that was set apart, as that promised to that peculiar peoples, as were rejected—as is shown in that portion when there is the turning back from the rising up of Xerxes as the deliverer from an unknown tongue or land, and again is there seen that this occurs in the entrance of the Messiah in this period—1998."

Here the reading stops. A continuation was given the following day, July 1.

"Much has been written respecting that represented in the Great Pyramid, and the record that may be read by those who would seek to know more concerning the relationships that have existed, that may exist, that do exist, between those of the Creative Forces that are manifest in the material world. As indicated, there were periods when a much closer relationship existed, or rather it should be said, there was a much better understanding *of* the relationship that *exists* between the creature and the Creator.

"In those conditions that are signified in the way through the Pyramid, as of periods through which the world has passed and is passing, as related to the religious or the spiritual experiences of man—the period of the present is represented by the low passage or depression showing a downward tendency, as indicated by the variations in the character of stone used. This might be termed in the present as the . . . age . . . in which preparations are being made for the beginning of a change, which—as indicated from the astronomical or numerical conditions—dates from the latter portion or middle portion of the present fall [1932]. In October there will be a period of in which the benevolent influences of Jupiter and Uranus will be stronger, which—from an astrological viewpoint—will bring a greater interest in occult or mystic influences.

"At the correct time accurate imaginary lines can be drawn from the opening of the Great Pyramid to the second star in the Great Dipper, called Polaris or the North Star. This indicates it is the system toward which the soul takes flight after having completed its sojourn through this solar system. In October there will be seen the first variation in the position of the polar star in relation to the lines from the Great Pyramid. The dipper is gradually changing, and when this change becomes noticeable—as might be calculated from the Pyramid—there will be the beginning of the change in the races. There will come a greater influx of souls from the Atlantean, Lemurian, La, Ur, or Da civilizations. These conditions are indicated in this turn in the journey through the Pyramid.

"How was this begun? Who was given that this should be a record of man's experiences in this root race? For that is the period covered by the prophecies in the Pyramid. This was given . . . in that period . . . when there were many who sought to bring to man a better understanding of the close relationship between the Creative Forces and that created, between man and man, and man and his Maker.

"Only those who have been called may truly understand. Who then has been called? Whosoever will make himself a channel may be raised to that of a blessing that is all that entity-body is able to comprehend. Who, having his whole measure full, would desire more does so to his own undoing.

"Q. 4. What are the correct interpretations of the indications in the Great Pyramid regarding the time when the present depression will end?

"A. 4. The changes as indicated and outlined are for the latter part of the present year [1932]. As far as depression is concerned, this is not—as in the minds of many—because fear has arisen, but rather that, when fear has arisen in the hearts of the created, *sin* lieth at the door. Then, the change will occur—or that seeking will make the definite change—in the latter portion of the present year. Not that times financially will be better, but the minds of the people will be fitted to the conditions better.

"Q. 5. What was the date of the actual beginning and ending of the construction of the Great Pyramid?

"A. 5. Was one hundred years in construction. Begun and completed in the period of Araaraart's time, with Hermes and Ra.

"Q. 6. What was the date B.C. of that period?

"A. 6. 10,490 to 10,390 before the Prince entered into Egypt.

"Q. 7. What definite details are indicated as to what will happen after we enter the period of the King's Chamber?

"A. 7. When the bridegroom is at hand, all do rejoice. When we enter that understanding of being in the King's presence, with that of the mental seeking, the joy, the

111

buoyancy, the new understanding, the new life, through the period.

"Q. 8. What is the significance of the empty sarcophagi?

"A. 8. That there will be no more death. Don't misunderstand or misinterpret! but the *interpretation* of death will be made plain.

"Q. 9. If the Armageddon is foretold in the Great Pyramid, please give a description of it and the date of its beginning and ending.

"A. 9. Not in what is left there. It will be as a thousand years, with the fighting in the air, and—as has been—between those returning to and those leaving the earth.

"Q. 10. What will be the type and extent of the upheaval in '36?

"A. 10. The wars, the upheavals in the interior of the earth, and the shifting of same by the differentiation in the axis as respecting the positions from the Polaris center.

"Q. 11. Is there not a verse of scripture in Isaiah mentioning the rock on which the Great Pyramid is builded?

"A. 11. Not as we find; rather the rock on which John *viewed* the New Jerusalem—that is, as of the entering in the King's Chamber in the Pyramid.

"Q. 12. What is the date, as recorded by the Pyramid, of entering in the King's Chamber?

"A. 12. '38 to '58.

"Q. 13. If the Passion of Jesus is recorded in the Great Pyramid, please give the date according to our present system of recording time?

"A. 13. This has already been presented in a fair and suitable manner through those students of same, and these descriptions have been presented as to their authenticity.

"Q. 14. How was this particular Great Pyramid of Gizeh built?

"A. 14. By the use of those forces in nature as make for iron to swim. Stone floats in the air in the same manner. This will be discovered in '58."

". . . With the storehouse, or record house (where the records are still to be uncovered) there is a chamber or passage from the right forepaw to this entrance of the record chamber, or record tomb. This may not be entered

112

without an understanding, for those that were left as guards may *not* be passed until after a period of their regeneration in the Mount. . . ."

IX

"THE RECORDS ARE ONE"

Elevators in the Gobi Desert!
A Poseidian temple near Bimini!
A blue vase from Ur!
These are some more of the tangible evidences of Atlantis which Cayce said were still around after 12,500 years, waiting to be discovered.

The specific directions, the intriguing hints, scattered among the readings are enough to make an archeologist grab his pick-ax and head for the nearest jet.

An aviatrix did just that back in 1935—headed for the nearest prop job, that is—and discovered a well with spooky inscriptions carved on it at Bimini.

Most of this fabulous collection of leads to new, important archeological finds has been left untouched.

Some of it has been partly uncovered, such as the Dead Sea Scrolls in Palestine: Cayce indicated that the scrolls' owners lived and taught at Mount Carmel. So far, little has been done there to prove or disprove this.

Matching and comparing lean and fat references, entire readings at times, we begin to see and to know the world as it was in 10,500 B.C., according to Cayce. This period was emphasized because it was the time of the breaking up of Atlantis, when migrations were going on and new nations were being born. Thus, this period is more sharply drawn for us than others Cayce described. Specific dates are offered marking events of that era. Prehistory was given not only for Egypt, but also for Yucatan and the Gobi Desert, for Persia, in many references given in individuals' life readings. In these cases, involving Yucatan, Gobi, and Persia, as well as Egypt, we have an amazingly consistent picture of their life and character in prehistoric times, which attest to high levels of culture.

An example of Cayce's plausibility in fixing the dates for this period is this list of historic events as culled from various readings:

The westward migration to Yucatan from Atlantis occurred around 10,600 B.C.

The city of Ur was flourishing from 10,500 B.C. to 10,420 B.C.—probably much earlier and much later as well, for these dates merely mark the time of one person's birth and death, in her individual reading.

The Great Pyramid of Gizeh was built from 10,490 B.C. to 10,390 B.C.

A library was established at Alexandria in 10,300 B.C.

The Gobi Desert's City of Gold, in the nation of Taoi, was a thriving metropolis in 10,000 B.C. and was contemporary with equally cultured nations of India, Norway, and Og (Peru).

The sprawling democracy of Taoi in the Gobi Desert of Mongolia and Northern China had its own independent and highly advanced civilization. There was an interchange of scientific, religious, and social ideas among these countries. Trade flourished among them, bringing "spices from India, cut stones from Egypt."

Cayce declared that the temple records that will be found in Egypt, Yucatan, and off Bimini will be found identical! In a reading on Mayan prehistory, he states: "Yet as time draws nigh when changes are to come about, there may be the opening of those three places where the records are one, to those that are the initiates in the knowledge of the One God.

"The Temple [built] by Iltar (Yucatan) will then rise again. Also, there will be the opening of the temple or hall of records in Egypt, and those records that were put into the heart of the Atlantean land may also be found there— that have been kept, for those that are of that group [Poseidia at Bimini].

"The *records* are *One*."

We can expect to find the artifacts in these three places to be similar.

But we cannot expect them to be marked "Made in Atlantis"! No. In fact, archeologists will be dealing with a whole new level of study that will probably take quite a while to carry out. We may be years in comparing the records and relics of the many sites yet to be excavated, if the exciting finds the future holds take as long to evaluate as have the Dead Sea Scrolls. We can envision a whole new generation of "Atlantologists" who will specialize in knowledge of that period. Certainly, it will take all the skills archeology has developed in recent decades to verify and explain the meaning of Atlantis.

Archeology has "grown up" in modern times. Its techniques were once haphazard, and in the process of digging, many people destroyed as much as they found. Now there are many scientific aids to make this an increasingly efficient science in itself. There are the carbon dating tests that can measure the age of a skull. There are new codebreaking techniques to decipher texts; more careful digging methods and labeling of artifacts; and lately, the use of X-rays to look inside such otherwise enigmatic structures as the Great Pyramid!

The Atlanteans used these very techniques, we conclude from Cayce's records, and they're back, to put their scientific know-how to work in every field! Cayce said that archeology was practiced in Egypt. If the people of that period had solar power and the laser, they were also pretty good archeologists.

In the overall picture Cayce presents, a pattern in man's development emerges, involving his innate need to remember, to preserve his identity and his past. Man needs his traditions to give him a sense of continuity and permanence. In knowledge of his history, he can better control the future and understand the present.

We enter the 1970's on the threshold of what can become for us and future generations "the best that's yet to be." This will be made clearer when "the records that are one" are found, and, with the record temples, or chambers that are opened, the minds and hearts of mankind in the twentieth century.

We note, the timing is perfect.

Bimini!

It is not the jewelry and the vases which archeologists

prize, however real they make the people of the past seem to us. It is rather the clay tablets, the parchments by which the past is communicated. We can expect that when the documents of Atlantis are found, they will represent a tremendous breakthrough for historians as well as scientists. However, Cayce's predictions come with the understanding that "yet as time draws nigh when changes are to come about, there may be the opening of these three places where the records are one, *to those that are the initiates in the knowledge of the One God.*" (Author's italics.)

What does this mean? Only that we will need to be spiritually mature, as well as scholarly, to appreciate the value of the discoveries in full. These will not be just another cache of exotic baubles. These will be the sacred relics of a God-fearing people who acknowledged Him above nationality and wealth. We do not begin to comprehend the powers they had in posting guards about the record chambers until they had been "regenerated in the mount." This is a mystery among many mysteries surrounding the Great Pyramid. But the Cayce readings have said that when the time is fulfilled, the right people will appear to undertake the opening of the records, and it will be by the hand of God.

Appropriately, the first inkling Cayce and his friends had of this trinity of sacred temples was in 1926 with the first mention of Bimini, which concerned nothing more important than oil wells. The Great Pyramid and the Hall of Records in Egypt was described in 1932. The idea of a "Temple of Iltar" at Yucatan was introduced in 1933.

Bimini! It consists of two very small islands among several thousand in the Bahamas, just forty-five miles east of the Miami coast and a haven for deep sea fishermen. But in 1926 when it first figured in the Cayce annals, it was virtually isolated and served chiefly as a station for rum-running.

Cayce described it as "the highest portion left above the waves of a once great continent, upon which the civilization as now exists in the world's history [could] find much of that as would be used as a means for attaining that civilization [Atlantis] . . ."

". . . for this is of the first highest civilization that will be

117

uncovered in some of the adjacent lands to the west and south of the isles, see?

"Q. 1. Was this the continent known as Alta or Poseidia?

"A. 1. A temple of the Poseidians was in a portion of this land.

"Q. 2. What minerals will be found there?

"A. 2. Gold, spar, and icthyolite."

This seems to indicate a temple of Poseidia is located in the vicinity of Bimini.

Besides, there's a lot of gold in those (underwater) hills, according to Cayce!

As may be surmised from various statements in the readings, not only Bimini itself, but the area to the south and west of it—the Gulf Steam—is the location of the new land to rise. This is part of the island of Poseidia, and "under the slime of the ages of sea water" near Bimini, part of the Poseidia temples may yet be discovered. With them, said Cayce, would be records like those in Egypt.

When land rises in this area, many "Atlanteans" will be drawn back to rebuild it! "There are, as has been given, many peoples being born again into the earth's plane who were, through their experiences, in this land. With the building, then, again, we find the innate desire will come to an innumerable number to be in some manner or way associated—either as dwellers for a portion of the time or the whole time, or as the investors in the project—to make this not only a habitable place, but as a resort equaled by none."

Other big things were suggested for Bimini. It could be made into a shipping port, with its many natural harbors and its convenient position on the waterways. It could become a strategic point in the affairs of several continents "as it has been in the eons past."

It could become a center for archeological research.

Hydroelectric power could be obtained from the tidal currents which "would supply all of the power necessary for any project that might be even undertaken here."

Bimini could be one of the biggest health resorts in the world. Cayce said that wells could be drilled there from which would flow the healing waters used by the Alanteans.

Was this, then, the legendary Fountain of Youth which Ponce de Leon came so close to finding?

There are actually two main islands of Bimini: North and South. The underground waters on these islands are very different, and yet both are excellent, according to Cayce. He said, "The northern portion of South Island will lend itself to the water supply—a sweet water—adaptable not only for the drinking purposes but for all purposes of the body. This will be found by drilling to the depth which will be, true enough, below the sea level, yet the source is from far, far away. Better water will be found (here) than in those lands known as the continents."

There are sulphur waters on the North Island: "The sulphur waters may be obtained where there is seen an old channel on north end of the south portion of the North Island. These will be of the black sulphur, yet for certain conditions, and for the baths as may be instituted through same, will be quite beneficial to health, and especially to those of the neuritic conditions—nervousness and the general rheumatic conditions, see? This will be found only eighty-nine to ninety feet deep."

But after the land around Bimini rises, the possibility of Bimini's becoming a resort, a shipping port, and all the rest changes. As the geologist author of *Earth Changes* remarked recently, this prediction seemed to indicate that Bimini's future as a resort and shipping center was limited to the time when there were opportunities for this.

Cayce did predict that a temple, its records matching those in Egypt, would be found. In fact, that there would be the remains of "temples" found in this part of Poseidia, when it appeared.

Where are these temples, or their ruins? Some one asked Cayce, "How deep in the ground will the [minerals and archeological remains] be found?"

"These will be found in the twelve to fifteen-foot levels," he said. "The vein, as workable, would be found extending in the northeast-southwest direction. . . ." These are below sea level.

Since "archeological remains" referred to in the record seem to indicate the temples Cayce had mentioned earlier, did Cayce mean that these would be found at the same level with the vein of gold?

Concerning the accuracy of the dating of the final destruction of Atlantis, the Geologist says that this might be determined by radiocarbon dating. A sample of mangrove peat encountered at a depth of nine feet below mean low water in a core boring on Bimini in 1957 was reported by Columbia University scientists to be 4,370 years old. "The date suggests that any materials encountered in the twelve to fifteen foot levels would be only a few thousand years older than about 4,372 years, and might possibly be of the order of 10,100 years or slightly more, the date given for final destruction of Atlantis."

Cayce's interest in Bimini began with a man who showed up with an apparently sincere sympathy for the work. He enlisted the clairvoyant's cooperation in trying to locate oil in Florida, promising that a hospital could finally be built from the proceeds of such a venture.

Edgar Cayce thus seemed drawn to this part of Poseidia by chance circumstances, without funds, but with a dream for healing his fellowmen fixed firmly in his heart and mind.

A whole series of readings followed the initial request for information on oil, Cayce directing operations in Florida from his couch in Virginia Beach. Several of the readings of pirate treasure which he said was also located there giving the precise location were never returned by his opportunistic friend, who disappeared shortly afterward.

But as was given in a reading on the work of Cayce: "Oft will it be learned by the study of phenomena of people's actions, that seemingly all forces in the universe are used to bring about that which is good, for it has been said, 'I will harden the heart of Pharaoh, that he will not let my children go.' Through this same seed came the Son of Man, and through these same trials through which the forefathers passed, the burdens and sins of the world were laid upon that Son.

"Then through the trials, the temptations, the besetters of evil from within and without, may any work that is His be expected to grow, and in that manner become polished bright, and a shining light unto the world; yet though He were the Son, He learned obedience through the things which He suffered."

In 1935 Melaney Freeman, a licensed pilot, learned of

the well of fresh water on Bimini and was curious.

"Edgar Cayce must have talked to her about this well in discussing Atlantis," noted Gladys Turner in this file, "because I can find nothing in her life reading mentioning it. Edgar Cayce had visited Bimini in February, 1927; possibly he heard a story from the natives about a supposed fresh water well which was visible at certain times with the flow of the tide."

Melaney decided to fly down to Bimini and look for herself. From Miami she wired Cayce: "Please send me directions to locate well in Bimini. Also sea tide incoming or outgoing best to get sample of water. Expect to go next week by plane for the day."

Cayce wired back, "Well in Bimini southeastern position of North Bimini. Tide only changes flow of well."

She found a fresh water well, she reported, marked or walled around the top with stones of peculiar composition and strange symbols. She asked in her next reading: "Could the well in Bimini be promoted and reconstructed?"

Cayce stated in reply that a center could be established for two purposes: regeneration from the well, and its surrounding waters for those who are ill, and a center for archeological research. "And as such actions [dredging for harbors] are begun, there will be found much more gold in the lands under the sea than there is in the world circulation today!"

"Aid may be found from the varied societies that have been founded for the geological and archeological activities . . . for much will be found. . . ."

There is that assurance again, despite Bimini's uncertain future, that "much will be found."

The Geologist who has done considerable work at Bimini, was unable to locate the well. Melaney Freeman said she found it below the water line on the southeastern part of North Bimini.

I asked Gladys Turner where Melaney Freeman is today, nearly thirty-three years later. Gladys stated that she had been out of touch with the aviatrix for a number of years, and has no way of locating her for help in rediscovering the well. Perhaps future excursions to Bimini by the Geologist and other researchers will yet yield knowledge about the well, the vein of gold, and those elusive Poseidian temples that lie beneath the sea!

Yucatan!

Among the Children of the Law of One, a certain Iltar led a group of ten people in one of many westward migrations to Yucatan in about 10,600 B.C. The Cayce readings indicate that these migrations were by air as well as by boat.

In Yucatan these Poseidians began a new civilization. They worked with those who had preceded them and others who had followed, keeping the spiritual tenets of their old homeland and building temples to their One God. They found here refugees from the Lemurian (Pacific) and Mu (lower California and Mexico) upheavals. Together they created a new culture—for the latter were equally anxious to preserve their religious principles. When the final upheavals in Atlantis occurred several hundred years later, much of the contour of the land in Central America and Mexico was changed to what it is now. Cayce stated that the first temples erected by Iltar and his followers were destroyed as this happened. But the temples which were built later by the combined peoples from "Mu, Oz, and Atlantis" were those which were being discovered at the time he gave the reading on this in 1933.

The most ancient and inscrutable pyramids in Mexico are at Teotihuacan, thirty-two miles from Mexico City. Here is located the Pyramid of the Sun, which is nearly as large as that called Gizeh in Egypt, but only 216 feet tall. Another was dedicated to the moon, and according to Ignatius Donnelly's Atlantis: *The Antediluvian World,** covers forty-five acres—or four times as much space as Gizeh. He cites the many similarities between the Mexican and the Egyptian monuments.

Donnelly states, "In Mexico pyramids were found everywhere. Cortez, in a letter to Charles V, states that he counted 400 of them at Cholula. Their temples were on those 'high places.'"

In reference to Cayce's statement that "the first temples

*New York: Harper & Row, Publishers, Inc.

that were erected by Iltar and his followers were destroyed" during the later upheavals, we would point out that Donnelly relays to us an observation of Bancroft that "In many of the ruined cities of Yucatan one or more pyramids have been found, upon the summit of which no traces of any building could be discovered, although upon surrounding pyramids such structures could be found . . ." He adds, however, that there is in Egypt another form of pyramid called the *Mastaba*, which, like the Mexican, was "flattened on the top" and is in fact found from Mesopotamia to the Pacific Ocean. These pyramids of Yucatan without temples could be of this order.

In her article, "Atlantis In Mexico," *Searchlight*, (June, 1963), Clare Templeton states that "there are some arresting comparisons with the Cayce readings" and the Toltecs, who some researchers think were the first high culture above the archaic level, and the originators of the calendar. The mass of legendary material about them is as heroic as it is confusing, but researchers agree that they did not practice human sacrifice. One legend which qualifies by sheer persistence is that they had airships and arrived in Mexico by this means. . . ." She states that the calendar stones, "on technical precision alone" are "more apt to be survivals from the earlier culture."

These pyramid ruins were also Incal in influence, though the Incals were themselves the successors of Oz or Og in the Peruvian land, and Mu. These same ruins were added to later, when there appeared on the scene members of the Lost Tribes of Israel! Thus these are remnants of Egyptian, Lemurian, Oz, and even Mosaic influences.

The Lost Tribes left Palestine three thousand years before Christ, and part of them came into Mu, or extreme southwestern United States, and then moved on to Mexico and Yucatan, centering in the area of Mexico City. Here arose a mixture of races again, and a different civilization.

Cayce referred to the civilization in Yucatan and Mexico as a "high" civilization, and that more than one such will be found as research progresses. But the Aztec people were a much later nation, which flowered around 1479 A.D. According to the Encyclopedia Britannica, "The word *Azteca* is derived from Aztlan (white land) where, according to the Aztec traditions, their tribe originated. . . . The Aztecs were people of the sun."

The Aztecs, however, were influenced by the Mosaic laws of human sacrifice, and combined the Atlantean worship of "God the Son" and the symbology of the *sun* with this later ideal of sacrifice, and sacrificed human beings—usually their enemies—to the sun! Cayce tells us that among the ruins in Yucatan are "the altars upon which there were the cleansings of the bodies of individuals (not human sacrifice; for this came much later with the injection of the Mosaic, and those activities of that area). These were later the altars upon which individual activities—that would today be termed hate, malice, selfishness, self-indulgence—were cleansed from the body through the ceremony. . . ."

We recall the ideals of the Temple of Sacrifice, in which the earlier Atlanteans sacrificed, said Cayce, not human beings, but their baser emotions. Thus the Aztecs applied these inherited concepts in degenerate form, offering their victims on the altars in great numbers to "keep the sun moving," as H. R. Hays tells us (*In the Beginnings,* G. P. Putnam's Sons, 1963).

In addition to the altars, Cayce said that further specific proof would be "the pyramids, the altars before the doors of the varied temple activities," an injection from the people of Oz and Mu.

The Aztec "Calendar Stone," which seems an interesting but primitive piece of gibberish, embodies, according to George C. Vaillant (*Aztecs of Mexico,* Doubleday and Co., 1941), a finite statement of the infinity of the universe." It was made in 1479 A.D., he states, and weighs over twenty tons. It is twelve feet in diameter.

Vaillant describes the relic thus: "In the center is the face of the Sun God, Tonatiuh, flanked by four cartouches which singly give the dates of the four previous ages of the world and together represent the date of our present era. The twenty names of the days circle this central element, and they, in turn, are ringed with a band of glyphs denoting jade or turquoise, which give the idea of being precious, and symbolize the heavens and their color. This strip is girdled by the signs for stars, through which penetrate designs emblematic of the rays of the sun. Two immense

Fire Serpents, symbolic of the year and Time, circle the exterior to meet face to face at the base. Boring back through these forms to the significance behind them, we have a grandiose conception of the majesty of the universe.

"According to Aztec belief," Vaillant adds, "the world has passed through four or five stages or Suns. Details differ, but the record on the great calendar Stone may be taken as the official version in Tenochtitlan. . . . Our present age, Four Earthquake, is under the control of the Sun God, Tonatiuh, and it will be destroyed, in time, by earthquakes."

But these beliefs are Aztec, you say. Not originally, according to Cayce. For he states that further evidence of the time of Atlantis were "the stones that are circular, that were of the magnetized influence upon which the Spirit of the One spoke to those peoples as they gathered in their service, are the earliest Atlantean activities in religious service, as would be called today."

Cayce speaks of another kind of stone—the "Great Crystal," a "large cylindrical glass" cut with facets so that the capstone on top of it controlled the power concentrated in it from the sun—the "firestone" of which he spoke in the data on Egypt. He says that in Yucatan there is the "emblem of same." This is stated to be the circular stone of the Aztecs (or their Atlantean forebears)—a *symbol* of the firestone. "Let's clarify this," Cayce continues, "for it may the more easily be found. For they will be brought to this America, these United States. A portion is to be carried, as we find, to the Pennsylvania State Museum. A portion is to be carried to the Washington preservation of such findings (Smithsonian Institute), or to Chicago."

Records as to how to construct the firestone will be found in Yucatan, Bimini, and Egypt. "As indicated, the records of the manners of construction of same are in three places in the earth, as it stands today: in the sunken portions of Atlantis, or Poseidia, where a portion of the temples may yet be discovered under the slime of ages of sea water, near what is known as Bimini, off the coast of Florida. And in the temple records that were in Egypt, where the entity later acted in cooperation with others in preserving the records that came from the land where these had been kept. Also the records that were carried to what is now Yucatan in America, where these stones (that they know so little about) are now—during the last few months—being uncovered." This was given December 20, 1933.

By way of Oz and Mu (or Peru and Mexico) the Lost Tribes injected their influence in the religious culture of Yucatan. "The pyramid, the altars before the doors of the varied temple activities, was an injection from the people of Oz and Mu; and will be found to be separate portions, and that referred to in the Scriptures as the high places of family affairs, family gods. . . ." Also, "The stones that are set in the front of the Temple, between the service temple and the outer court temple" were later adopted by the Hebrews in their worship.

There still remains a temple of Iltar in Yucatan, where the records are waiting to be discovered. As for what happened to Iltar's later people, we are told "Those in Yucatan, those in the adjoining lands as begun by Iltar, gradually lost in their activities (through generations); and came to be that people termed, in other portions of America, the Mound Builders."

But Yucatan, Bimini, and Egypt are not the only places where there may be found evidences of Atlantis. Cayce added other places in the following statement: "The position the continent Atlantis occupied is between the Gulf of Mexico on one side and the Mediterranean on the other. Evidences of Atlantean civilization may be found in the Pyrenees and Morocco and in British Honduras, Yucatan and parts of the Americans—especially near Bimini and in the Gulf Stream in this vicinity."

X

TAOI!

Thousands of miles east of Atlantis, on the vast plains of Mongolia, in 10,000 B.C. throve a nation covering 102,000 square miles.

What fabulous secrets now lie hidden under the sands of the barren wastelands of the Gobi Desert? In this part of the world which has seen little geologic change in centuries, gazelles graze and fierce winds howl. Beneath the sparse growth of sagebrush and thorn, says Cayce, one day will be found the fabulous City of Gold—Taoi!

A prophecy in 1935 linked Alexandria, Yucatan and Gobi, as archeological "interests that are arising in the . . . unearthing—as in Alexandria, as it will be in Yucatan, as is to be in the next two and one-half years in the Gobi. . . ."

Just what archeological research went on in the Gobi at that time (1937) is not clear. Certainly no City of Gold has yet been reported found there. At the time of the readings, archeologists had been working at Angyang, south of Peking, under Chinese and American auspices. Civil War stopped it in 1930, vandalism by grave robbers hampered later attempts, and by 1937 the Japanese were invading North China. However, says H. R. Hays in *In the Beginnings,* "Despite interruptions during the war with Japan, the fall of Chiang Kai-shek and the formation of the People's Republic, excavation of sites in North China has gone on since 1928 until we can form a picture of a great culture as significant and sophisticated as that of Mesopotamia or Egypt."

Judging from Edgar Cayce's dissertation on the pre-history of the Gobi Desert, the civilization of Taoi shared that status, and it still remains to be one of the major discoveries of the future.

Cayce said Taoi had been peopled by migrations from Lemuria, more as a latter-day contemporary of that civilization than as a refugee center. It was thus influenced by this early advanced race, about whom very little is given in the Cayce files. Taoi became "among the highest state of advancement in material accomplishments for the benefit or conveniences for man's indwelling. . . ." As a colony (?) of Lemuria and as a nation in its own right, it was led by the ruler Mu, the "prophet, the sage, the lawgiver."

Among the materials used for construction, we are told, were precious woods and metals: "And here, as may be discovered when these are excavated, the greater use of timbers or wood as a building material was exercised. . . ." He adds that there was constructed a "temple of gold—overlaid—its beams, its walls, its panelings—with many colored polished woods."

This was a very democratic nation with democracy extending into its religious practices. The people gathered in a temple "for speech-making. There were no priests as in many other lands." They *all* spoke and had what "would be called a forum, such as a group known in thine own land as the Quakers—who spoke when they were moved by, not anxiety, not wrath, but by the spirit of thoughtfulness—or the recognizing of Mind, the Builder. But the laborer was heard as well as those that were of every trade as would be termed in the present."

Cayce states: "There was equality between the sexes during that experience. There was only, as has been indicated, monogamy; not polygamy *ever* practiced among these peoples. The rights of each were the rights of the other. When by injury, wrath, accident, the mate was destroyed or killed, or by [natural] death, then the choice was made by the individual and seconded by those that were in the authority as to judgments. But those that judged were as the common people, as those in authority. For only the Prince, only those of the household of the Prince, were the 'last word'—but they never as lords, priests, presidents or dictators, but as interpreters of the law between man and man! And all interpreters were of the law between man and man! And all interpreters were moved to speech, or moved by the spirit in that ye call religion in the present, though these later—with the mixing of those from India and especially from Caucasia—made for disturbances in the second generation after Muzuen."

Muzuen was the name of the son of Mu, or the Prince who was the same as the person for whom this reading was given by Cayce. He took his place as heir to the throne at the age of sixteen and proved to be an enlightened ruler, a "prepared pacifist." He unified his country and later saw the development of explosives for defense.

During his time there occurred "the destruction of the mighty forests to the north, upon what are now the mountains of lime, salt, and sodas."

Muzuen was described as "five feet eleven. Blue of eye. Hair dark gold. Six fingered; five toed."

(Six fingered?)

"In dress: leather, linen, cotton, silk—in their varied seasons, their varied activities. Not given to ornaments as much as many, and this gradually turned the peoples from personal adornment to their home, their cities, their recreation places, their preparations for defense, their preparation for offense."

Adornments included "the finer works in laces, fabrics, spun gold, silver, carved ivory, and the like."

Elsewhere, the people are described as wearing clothing of "flax, cotton, ramie, silk" and using articles made of "gold, silver, lead, radium."

They had also a technology like ours, for they had electricity. They even had elevators! Cayce declared that there will be found here "lifts or elevators, the one-line electrical car, the very fast aerial locomotion—these were a portion of these experiences. . . ."

"The communications—not the telegraph as is known today; more of that of the voice transmission of quite a different type and nature."

"As to the manner of defense and offense, as has been indicated, much that is yet to be found again was a part of those preparations in those periods. For these then had to do with the setting of long-period drums for defense in which there might be any attempts by others to interfere, to cause their *own* undoing."*

Although Cayce does not say so, we can probably expect that gold coins which the people used as means of exchange will be found at Taoi. These he described as being "edged or etched; but no figures, no individual heads. These came later. But *holes* in same; almost square pieces, strung." The square coins were thus notched—"smooth but edged that it might be known from other groups that gradually used the same—and was changed to this when it was found that the Atlanteans' were almost the same." They were "strung to be worn about the waist or about the neck."

As each labored, said Cayce, as each saved, each received from a common storehouse, a common bank. There was no Government Bank and no taxation. Everyone worked, including the women and children, and all were paid the same: a piece of gold for a day's labor, for all did what they could. It was "all for the one, and one for all."

In trading with other countries the same coins were used.

Gold existed in fabulous quantities: "For with the City of Gold there will be found—well, there is not so much now even in the treasury or vaults of the U.S.A.!" There was much pomp, much use of gold trappings in the heraldry—"for gold was then as the sands to these peoples."

Unimpressed by gold except for ornament and as a means of exchange, these people had great regard for the religious life. One person was told he had been a missionary to Taoi, and had built a temple as the "representation of the understandings in the moral, the mental, the religious and spiritual life."

Another was told that he had helped with the "Temple Beautiful that was established in Taoi which may some day be brought to light . . . when there have been those concentrated efforts in the direction to uncover the activities that will make for a greater correlating of the fact that Truth is

*This is explained in Chapter XII.

that which grows in the hearts of men to make them aware of their relationships to their Maker. . . ."

A woman was told that she had ministered to the needs of the peoples in "the Temple", providing "ointments, lotions, odors," which were typical aids for worship at the altars of that time.

What will be found of the democracy of Taoi, one day? Elevators in the Gobi Desert? Gold coins that are square? A city of gold? And if these people preserved their dead as did the Egyptians, perhaps the mummy of Prince Muzuen will be found—with those twelve fingers!

Indo-China

Thailand and Cambodia were in the world news early in November, 1967, when Mrs. Jacqueline Kennedy visited there to fulfill a childhood dream—that of seeing ruins of the ancient Cambodian city of Angkor. Here is the largest religious building in the world, the Angkor Wat.

And there is another "City of Gold" to be discovered, said Cayce, in Thailand.

Evidence of a life in "Siam or Indo-China" was promised one person when "there will one day be opened the proof of those activities and experiences of that person there; the proofs of what this entity, with the companion, wrought in the experiences of the people of that land—that caused eventually those changes in the trend westward of what man has called civilization!

"A whole city—yes, a temple—will be uncovered, as will be the City of Gold in the Gobi land."

Such "proofs" suggest that here may be found, as in Egypt, tombs or buildings containing written documents which will bear an account of a remote history of that people. Whether the time was 10,000 B.C. or 100 B.C. is not even hinted at. The only clue is that the people referred to somehow caused changes to come about in the westward trend of civilization. This sounds as if we might place it only in prehistoric times.

"Thailand," whose name means "land of the free," has enjoyed centuries of independence. It is located in Indochina, between Burma and Cambodia, and bordered on the northeast by Laos. Its central region is a fertile river basin of farmland and among the mountain valleys to the north are more farmlands, growing rice, tropical fruits, and vegetables. The present people are originally from China; their religion, Buddhist.

Cayce made reference to another city "in Indo-China, where there are uncoverings even now of the city in which the entity resided." More combinations of iron will be found here, according to another reading.

But where is that City of Gold of old Siam?

Lemuria

Lemuria, which was destroyed before Atlantis, is not so clearly drawn for us among the Cayce records. He told one person that she was among those who established a temple of worship near what was her birthplace in this life, or Santa Barbara, California. This, he said, "must in the near future fade again into those joinings with the land of Mu"—that is, sink into the Pacific with the Lemurian inundations.

We find few evidences of the Lemurian civilization suggested for future excavation, except those which were left by peoples who came from that continent, mixing with other peoples, such as at Gobi or Yucatan.

One instance, however, stands out. A man was told he had come from Mu "when there were being those banishments and preparations for the preserving; for they had known that the land must soon be broken up."

This person was "among those that journeyed from Mu to what is now Oregon; and there still may be seen something of the worship as set up, in what was the development from that set up by the entity . . . as the totem or family tree."

In other words, the totem pole is a direct "descendant" of Mu. Another equally intriguing lead is indicated off lower California, where a "Princess Shu-Tu" of Lemuria journeyed "to see, to know." Here may be found a certain Canyon Island which "will be a part of the discoveries of . . . natural formations.

"For *this* was the entity's place of the temple."

132

XI

CARMEL: A SCHOOL OF PROPHETS

In the northwestern corner of Palestine, in Haifa on Mount Carmel, stands a Carmelite monastery, a thriving center which includes a church, a school, and a shrine of the early Carmelite monks.

A quarter of a mile away at Wadi es Siah are the ruins of the *first* monastery of this order, the place where Elijah was supposed to have started the order known as the Sons of the Prophets who lived to prepare their community for the birth of the Messiah. Here are a garden spot and a cave which has a famous spring—Elijah's Spring. Still another spot is supposed to be where Elijah slew the four hundred priests of Baal.

Another cave and spring revered by the Jews is located at a distance from the first, on the northwest side of Carmel, and is also claimed to be that of the prophet.

Scattered over the entire mount, which is shaped like a loaf of bread, are the unexplained ruins of entire cities.

Although scholars have not yet linked this place with the community of Qumram, one hundred fifty miles away, where the Dead Sea Scrolls were found in 1947, the Edgar Cayce readings abundantly suggest that Mount Carmel was the original "School of the Prophets" of the people of Qumram, and furthermore, that an Essene Temple was located there at the time of Jesus.

This mass of evidence is to be found in what is known as the "Palestine Readings." We have here without doubt predictive material that can be compared with the Dead Sea Scrolls, and that was given the world ten years before the scrolls were found! Will the Temple of the Essenes at

Mount Carmel perhaps be found some day? This will be for the archeologists to answer.

Twenty years ago seven of a vast library of parchments were discovered—scrolls written by an obscure Jewish sect, the Essenes, who lived at the time of Jesus. These were followed by lesser finds in later years. Among the first was a *Manual of Discipline,* which tells of the Essenes' communal life at Qumram. Others found with it included the Book of Isaiah, a commentary on the Book of Habakkuk, and an addition to Genesis written in Aramaic. The scrolls were in various states of disintegration and had to be reassembled before they could be edited and published.

Bibles in use today, based on manuscripts dating only to the ninth century, have thus come to be questioned by scholars who are comparing them with the original manuscripts.

The Essenes were destroyed by the Romans in the first century A.D., but before their dispersal they collected their precious library of important records and teachings of the prophets, which date from 100 B.C. or earlier, put them into large jars, and hid them in the caves of Qumram. Although the sect was destroyed, the scrolls were kept from utter decay by the fortunate climatic conditions prevalent there.

Information gleaned from the giant work of assembling the badly fragmented scrolls for editing and publishing is eagerly awaited by Christians and Jews for the new insight into their histories it will bring. The scrolls are termed by some scholars as "revolutionary," written on the eve of Christianity and therefore of more authority than those produced later.

Of major importance already is the contribution which the Essenes made to Christianity. According to certain of the scrolls, the Essenes were a people "set apart" from the Pharisees and Sadducees at the time of Jesus. Their communal and ascetic life, their persecution at the hands of the Romans, and their adherence to a form of Judaism which later paved the way for Christianity, are vividly set forth.

The Essenes are not mentioned either in the Old Testament or the New. But what the Dead Sea Scrolls reveal about them was indicated and anticipated in the Cayce records as early as 1936. Their daily lives, studies, customs, all centering around the Holy Family, were set forth in great detail in readings given for many people allegedly associated with the Master during His life on earth.

The Cayce readings state that the Essenes provided the social and religious setting into which Jesus was born, that their goal, years before Jesus' birth, was preparing a fit community into which the Messiah could be born. The meaning of *Essene,* the readings state, is "expectancy."

These were a dedicated people and evidently existed only to nurture this great Event into the world, as their existence is not recorded for us in the orthodox sources of the present day.

Exquisite insight is given into the hearts and minds of Mary, Joseph, and many others surrounding them. Of special interest are those who helped Joseph and Mary in the care and teaching of Jesus at Mount Carmel, in the Temple. It was in the Temple, also, that Mary was chosen, and it was there that she and Joseph were married.

Essenism has been known to scholars through the works of Pliny, Josephus, and Philo. Now the Dead Sea Scrolls will give us new understanding of the beginnings of Christianity. They will be confirmed by another approach: the Edgar Cayce readings.

A typical reading from the Palestine group was given June 27, 1937:

"In the days when more and more leaders of the people had been trained in the temple at Mount Carmel—the original place where the school of prophets was established during Elijah's time—there were those leaders called Essenes who were students of what ye would call astrology, numerology, phrenology, and the study of the return of individuals, or reincarnation.

"There were certain reasons why these proclaimed that certain periods formed a cycle—reasons which grew out of the study of Aristotle, Enos, Mathias, Judah and others who supervised the school, as you would term it.

"These men and women had been persecuted by leaders of the people, and this had caused the saying of which ye have an interpretation, as given by the Sadducees, 'There is no resurrection' or 'There is no reincarnation'—which is what the statement meant in those periods.

"In the lead of these reasons were those changes . . . from the position of the stars . . . that stand, as it were, at the dividing of the ways between the universal vision of the solar system and those from outside the spheres. The North Star in its variation made for those cycles, and this began the preparation for the three hundred years, as has been given. Then in these signs was the new cycle which was . . . the beginning of the Piscean Age—of the position of the Polar or North Star, as related to the southern clouds . . .

"These, then, were the beginnings. Then there was the prophecy of old which had been handed down from the experiences of the sages of old—that an angel was to speak. When this occurred at the choosing of the maiden who (as known only by those close to her) had been immaculately conceived, the preparation of the Mother was brought to a focal point."

"In the Faith of the Fathers"

"Much might be given as to the how, why, and when of the purposes that brought about the materialization of Jesus in the flesh.

"In giving then, the history: There were those in the faith of the fathers to whom the promises had been given that they would be fulfilled as from the beginning of man's record.

"Hence there was a continued preparation and dedication of those who might be the channels through which this chosen vessel might enter—through choice—into materiality.

"Thus in Carmel, where there were the priests of this faith, there were the maidens chosen who were dedicated to this purpose, this office, this service. Among them was Mary, the beloved, the chosen one; and she, as had been foretold, was chosen as the channel. Thus she was separated and kept in closer associations with and in the care of this office.

"That was the beginning, that was the foundation of what ye term the Church.

136

"Then, when the days were fulfilled that the prophecy might come that had been given by Isaiah, Malachi, Joel, and those of old, she, Mary, espoused to Joseph, a chosen vessel for the office among those of the priests, the sect or group who had separated and dedicated themselves in body, in mind, in spirit for this coming—became with child."

Jesus' Childhood and Training

"There was a period of purification according to the law, then the days in the temple and the blessing by Anna and by the high priest. And these constituted the early days of the beginning of the entity called Jesus, who becomes the Christ, the Master of Masters. During this period there was the return to Nazareth and then the edict that sent them into Egypt so that the prophecy might be fulfilled, 'My son shall be called from Egypt.'

"There five years were spent, as you term time, by the mother, Joseph and the child. Then there was the return to Judea and to Capernaum, where dwelt many of those who later were the closer companions of the Master.

"Here, after the period again of presentation at the temple, when there were certain questionings among the leaders, the Entity was sent first—again—into Egypt for only a short period, and then into India, and then into what is now Persia.

"Hence, the Entity was trained in all the ways of the various teachers.

"From Persia He was called to Judea at the death of Joseph, and then into Egypt for the completion of His preparation as a teacher. He was with John, the messenger, during a portion of His training there in Egypt.

"Then He returned to Capernaum, Cana, and there came the periods of first preparation, in the land of His nativity.

"The rest ye have according to Mark, John, Matthew and Luke; these in their order record most of the material experiences of the Master.

"Many details may be given as to the varied fields of preparation, but these were the main experiences."

Jesus' first teacher, Josie, was Mary's handmaid. Mary and Josie knew the Mosaic law and the Prophets, as well as the mysteries of astrology. They were by no means ignorant of the culture of their world and they taught the Boy entrusted to their care until He was twelve, when He was sent to the prophetess, Judy. This woman taught Him "the prophecies" and at sixteen He was sent to Persia and then to India. After that, He went to Egypt to be taught by the temple priests.

The myriad of data given for the people who had experiences in Palestine would be too much to present here, but the quotations given here afford some glimpses into the wealth of material that one day should be compared with the Dead Sea Scrolls.

The prophetess Judy figures large in the Cayce panorama of events surrounding the life of the Master, because her influence did not end with her guiding Jesus' education, but continued throughout long years following His death, among the Essenes and the early Christians. Perhaps her records are among the Scrolls, for she not only helped to shape events, but she recorded them, as well. These records were studied first at Carmel, then by the other Christian communities, including Antioch, Jerusalem, Smyrna, and Philadelphia (Amman).

Bible Land Prophecies

Tombs of Theresa and Herod the Great

One woman was told she had been Theresa, the Roman Queen of Palestine, wife of Herod the Great. She lived from 28 B.C. to 6 A.D.

In 1940 she asked, "Can I find my name Theresa written in any history?"

Said Edgar Cayce: "Best to find it written in the tablets in the burial places about Jerusalem. There it will be found, as with The Great."

She was writing then a book as yet unpublished on the Palestine Period, drawn to this because as Theresa she had been sympathetic to the Essenes and secretly had helped their cause. In that life she was murdered after the death of her husband, upon his previous orders.

She now asked Cayce, "What should be the title, purpose, and general outline of this book on the Palestinian Period?"

"The Dawn of a New Day (or Era): the needs of the world for the new message, which is in keeping with the needs in the present—as then. There was the looking forward to the coming of the Prince of Peace, the new era. These are before you, even as then. These presentations would make same timely."

Nor have the tombs of Herod and Theresa yet been found. Now that the Israelis again control Jerusalem, perhaps they will attempt the archeological excavation that will lead to this important find.

An Essene bishop evidently traveled as far as Chaldea to establish a church. According to a reading about him, documents bearing his sermons will be found near Ur of the Chaldees.

A young girl of twenty-one was told that she should wear a replica of King David's seal, and she asked where she could find such an article.

She had psychic powers, Cayce told her, so that it would be easy for her to make a seal that would be correct in design. The original "will one day be uncovered in Jerusalem" and "could be duplicated in either ivory, coral, or gold."

This is another discovery which will create great excitement and will be of great meaning to both Christians and Jews.

More records will be found in Iran, or Persia, following excavations which will uncover stores and records which were put there by one Artial. This prediction was given in 1927. Another prediction states that in the Arabian desert, near Shuster, lie the ruins of a city that will soon be discovered. Among the temple ruins will be "the dressings for the altar—or as would be called the accoutrements of the altar service that was carried on there."

When this city existed and when it will be discovered

were not given. One reference to this was given August 7, 1926.

And then there was the lady who was told that her vase had just turned up in Ur after 12,500 years! Cayce said that in recent excavations in old Ur, where she had lived from 10,500 to 10,420 B.C., there was a vase "where there is the piper, with the drawing of the chariot" that had been among her own possessions. "It's blue in color," he added.

Africa

Far to the south of Egypt, where the Nile has its beginnings, is Ethiopia, a mountainous plateau with peaks ranging to fifteen thousand feet in height. The emperor of this ancient land boasts that he descends from Solomon and the Queen of Sheba. These people have been isolated from the world by their mountains until the 1930's and archeology reportedly has not yet come upon the hieroglyphics which Edgar Cayce says are there: ". . . There still may be seen in some of the mountain fastnesses of that land, particularly in the Upper Nile where there were those activities in the mountains, the images of the entity that are often worshipped . . . [and] the entrance to the tombs there.

"Then the name was Ai-Ellain and the hieroglyphics will be found to be marked as these: The Ibex (the bird of same), the hornheaded man, the Ibex turned in the opposite direction, the sacred bull of Ipis [?], the hooded man as of the Ethiopian people, the cross, the serpent (upright), the staff with the symbol (that should be the symbol of the entity through its experience) as the B's turned towards each other . . . or one upright with two loops on either side of same, with the serpent head two ways from the top of same . . ."

Such a discovery, were it to take place, would link Egypt with Ethiopia by inscriptions, images, and tombs, as well as by the ever-constant Nile.

Opposite Ethiopia on the African map is the little country of Liberia on the west coast. It was founded for Negro slaves—escaped refugees from the United States in 1822—and is covered by tropical rain forests which repel travel. In the southernmost part, says Cayce, is "a city upon top of the city" and much may be found of a school established there by another refugee, of another time: one in exile from Egypt at the time of Atlantis!

This school taught the "ideal realtionships between individuals," and its leader disseminated "the tenets and laws in many lands."

In this city may be found the name *Cubri,* the man's name in that life, according to Cayce.

XII

THE PRISM

"All power is from one Source: God." Edgar Cayce thus put on an equal basis the laws that govern material science with those that govern spiritual realities. In this orderly universe, everything has its place and its function. The same God which says "Love is law . . . law is love" on the spiritual level, tells us "Matter doesn't change in chemical transformation" on the scientific level.

Cayce used the example of a prism separating the rays of light. The various colors thrown out are like the various aspects of the universal laws, but all from the same source. These laws become manifest in our material world as we develop our sciences and gain knowledge of their existence.

"All such laws," he predicted, "as man develops, will come to the use and benefit of man, there being many illustrations in the present age."

That was January, 1925.

Cayce described the use of these laws by the Atlanteans and said that they were being rediscovered. From this same fundamental Source are derived the laws described in the chapter "Destiny and the Law." It was because the Atlanteans abused these that they were doomed. This age is subject to the same rules because they are eternal.

Some of the important scientific discoveries based on these eternal principles, said Cayce, would be those which have since been recognized by students of the readings as the laser, solar power, hydroelectric power, electromagnetic power, infrasound (see p. 151).

Cayce also described techniques of healing which sometimes had nothing to do with medicine or surgery and are so simple and mild as to make us doubt their effectiveness. His many physical readings reflected, not one limited approach to healing, but all agencies within the powers of man to employ. Healing by electrotherapy, healing by light, infrared-rays, shortwave, physiotherapy, diet, vitamins, packs, oil rubs, poultices, osteopathy, were what worked for his patients, and in this they were predictive of what modern medicine will hopefully acknowledge in the future.

Surgery was often bypassed in his suggested treatments, in favor of these other techniques. They were prescribed, too, as preventive measures, for the saying that "Prevention is better than cure" was an underlying philosophy. Cayce was, however, quick to suggest surgery when it was really needed.

The Physiotherapy Research Division

The clear-eyed, ruddy-faced man stood on a slope of the hill outside the A.R.E. headquarters building and vigorously led a breathless group of young people through a stretching exercise.

"Hands above heads—good!" Silently, the motley collection of "athletes" followed through.

"Circular motion with your body . . . now bend forward. Breathe in and through the nostrils, as you rise on your toes. That's right! Now breathe deeply!"

He paused; they breathed.

"Exhale quickly through your mouth, not through your nose . . ."

Sounds of exhalation nobly accomplished.

It was a recent summer day and a lot had happened since Dr. Harold J. Reilly first heard of a Cayce reading. That had been forty years ago, when physiotherapy was young. Reilly is founder and head of the Reilly Health Service, Rockefeller Center, New York. He has worked in the field of physiotherapy and drugless therapy since 1916.

He first heard of Cayce when a patient of the latter was referred to him. He has been working with the Cayce suggestions ever since, and has lectured on them many times to audiences in many cities.

In the summer of 1967 the Edgar Cayce Foundation announced the formation of a Physiotherapy Research Division with Dr. Reilly as director. He has donated to the Foundation specialized equipment used by the Health Service. With the equipment, students are being trained in the Cayce-Reilly methods at the clinic set up in the basement of the headquarters at Virginia Beach.

The Cayce-Reilly methods include exercise, manipulation, hydrotherapy, and application of light, heat, electricity. Later, these kinds of therapy will be researched with members of the Association.

Dr. Reilly is a trustee of the Edgar Cayce Foundation and the author of two books, *The Secret of Better Health* and *Easy Does It*. In a *Searchlight* article once, he described the progress physiotherapy has made since it was discovered fifty years ago.

This healing art was developed by the Army during World War II, Reilly explains, when many boys back from the battlefields needed whatever help they could get.

Amazingly predictive in respect to this field is the fact that the therapies now in use were described by Cayce in detail forty years ago! "There was no chance at that time (1924-1929) of Edgar Cayce's having been familiar with these types of physiotherapy, yet he gave readings containing electrotherapy, short wave, and ultra short wave," he states.

"Even now I can take the latest findings in the field of physiotherapy and compare them with readings given forty years ago and I assure you the readings do not come out second best! For instance, a famous Russian scientist and several of the other experts on longevity and geriatrics have said that the average age of man should be about 140 years. In one of the Cayce readings, a question was asked about old age. The answer was that if the person lived properly, ate properly, didn't worry too much and kept an optimistic outlook on life, he could live to be 120 years of age.

"So the facts that we continually get from scientific sources, and facts given in the readings, can more and more often be reconciled."

144

Another man who is working with the Edgar Cayce Foundation to further its research in healing is William A. McGarey, M.D., who, as head of the Foundation's Medical Research Division, Phoenix, Arizona, spent six weeks during the summer of 1967 in this endeavor. He conducted a study of the research program and, on the basis of his work over the past ten years with the readings, sent a letter to interested physicians throughout the country to enlist their cooperation in the use of the concepts in the readings.

"The medical concepts and treatments contained in many thousands of the Edgar Cayce readings have frequently proved to be remarkably effective," writes Dr. McGarey in this letter. "This has led to a demand reflected in scores of the letters received at the Headquarters of the Association for Research and Enlightenment, Inc., for advice and help in receiving aid of a medical nature embodying the knowledge imparted through the Edgar Cayce readings."

He requests physicians to accept as patients those A.R.E. members seeking help from the readings. The Foundation will furnish data from the readings as it is requested by member patients.

In conversation with Dr. McGarey this summer, I asked him why the medical profession has been so slow to research such healing agencies as suggested in the Cayce data.

"A scientist, it seems to me, either accepts the reality of God or rejects it," he said. "The scientist who rejects the reality of a creative God cannot come to a satisfactory understanding of the energies as they are existent. He may measure the energies, but this is like taking measurement of a house and never taking consideration of the materials, the people who built it, the architect who makes the plans."

I asked him about appliances for healing by electric current.

He pointed out that there has been in the past a sporadic, insignificant interest in the healing properties of electric currents. He feels that the use of this principle—low-voltage electrical impulses which are sent through the body—is a legitimate means of healing.

145

"It's described in a book by L.E. Eeman—the only other authority I have seen about it," he told me.

I looked up the book—*Cooperative Healing* by Eeman, published in 1947 in England. It tells of "experiments which can be repeated at will and of facts which can be controlled and measured by instruments." Basically, it seems to describe experiments using electrical current for healing.

In France, Russia, and Japan, electrical current is sweeping the population! According to a report in the November, 1967 issue of the *Ladies' Home Journal,* no one in those countries is waiting for science to research this method of healing. The people there are going ahead and using it, not for the entire body, just the head.

Bob Gaines states in his feature "You and Your Sleep" (*Ladies Home Journal,* Nov. 1967), "In France and Japan, insomniacs drop into local drugstores to pick up tiny, transistorized gadgets with electrodes that send a mild electric current through their heads. In the Soviet Union, there are 300 'sleep stations,' where patients in beds are plugged into a communal electrical outlet. It's not electrocution, it's electrosleep—and it's becoming the rage of Europe. Partisans claim it can produce the equivalent of a night's sleep in two hours and can cure everything from schizophrenia to ulcers. Somehow, the small current is supposed to cause a beneficial electrical discharge from the brain. The Russians claim seventy-five percent of all patients at the sleep stations rest better after treatment.

"American sleep researchers are uncertain. Our foremost electrosleep authority is Dr. Sigmund Forster of Maimonides Hospital in New York City. Forster's objection is that no one knows what happens when current goes through the brain. 'It could easily be the power of suggestion that makes people sleep when the machine's on.'

"At the moment, no one in the U.S. is using electrosleep equipment for anything other than experiments. You'll probably have to fly to Moscow if you want to get *really* charged up for the night."

As a key to understanding this form of healing, the following reading is important, though not among the material relegated to physical healing techniques. It is, in

146

fact, from a reading on "psychic healing," an entirely separate field covered at length in the readings, yet containing basic ideas related to electric current healing.

"Each atomic force of a physical body is made up of its units of positive and negative forces, that brings it into a *material* plane. These are of the ether, or atomic forces, being electrical in nature. . . ."

Is this a clue as to how electric current could heal the body?

Like so many other suggestions of a unique nature in these files, this has a predictive quality. The report that "electrosleep" is the rage in Europe, claiming cures for "everything from schizophrenia to ulcers" surely seems to be a fulfillment of this particular suggestion.

What is Healing?

No healing, said Cayce, is perfected without some psychic force exerted.

In the reading in which he said the body was made up of electrical, atomic units, Cayce said further that Jesus while on earth only used the "universal law," which implies that he made this manifest "in the last overcoming even the disintegration of the spirit and soul from the physical or corporal body. . . ."

So Jesus was "able to force all law to become subjugated (by His will) to the body, or, as shown in the electrical forces as used by man." He demonstrated for us that "the body is only atoms in motion and was able to heal others (to raise the dead) to raise Himself after death, and to become proof thereby that physical and spiritual laws emanate from the one Source."

This is applicable to more than psychic healing. The entire man is involved in his well-being—his emotions, his attitudes, even his purpose in life. Doctors in recent years have become aware not only of the physical nature of healing, but of the many other aspects, including marital, vocational and social problems, which create the total health picture. Cayce predicted this, for he said that one's emotions could make him sick or well. Moreover, he advised that the person caring for an ill person should be one who "exerted psychic force" by prayer, and a loving and sympathetic rapport with his patient, for the best healing results.

Immunity to the Law?

Sometimes, in working with the laws of which Cayce spoke, people close to the readings became puzzled because they still didn't understand that the laws work on various levels. As was pointed out, the laws are of the same Source, but they operate true to their function, and within the realm they govern.

But when it comes to the matter of praying for others, isn't one immune to physical ailments, protected and guarded by one's love for others?

"Why should one develop organic trouble while praying for his fellow man?" asked one person, herself suffering perhaps from a disability, and dismayed that this should happen in spite of her sincere prayer life.

"A natural consequence of being in organic matter," answered Cayce. "There are laws in organic influences that are seen through the natural chemical reaction, and those that pertain to the natural forces or environs; for under whatever environ an individual is, it is subject to the laws of that!"

This is a very important key, we believe, in separating the laws as to their various levels, for a better understanding of them. We are in a physical environment and a physical body which needs physical care, and we are subject to the laws of that body. That we work in the spiritual realm, also, using the laws of prayer and meditation, does not necessarily mean we are freed from the physical laws, themselves divine, after all! The approach to physical laws in the Cayce readings is a step up in our human concept of spirituality, for it holds that all laws are divine.

The only law that does intervene for us, in our karmic pattern, is the Law of Grace, and in this, all may be forgiven, even as we forgive, and we may be absolved from our debts because Christ died for us.

But otherwise, the laws are strict and operate without change—or they would not be divine laws!

How good it is to know that they do work, as demonstrated for us in the physical world plainly enough! From this, we can learn to respect the spiritual laws and to realize that they are not to be broken, but are to be understood and lived by, for the good of all.

Research

Research to a limited degree has been done on the Edgar Cayce readings, on such diverse subjects as epilepsy, the use of castor oil packs, multiple sclerosis, the use of Glycothymoline, pyorrhea and leukemia, says Dr. McGarey. Many doctors have reported favorably on cases brought to Cayce. In recent years, a medical doctor studied all the readings on four different diseases—multiple sclerosis, pyorrhea, leukemia, and epilepsy—and evaluated them for future researchers. The readings had given unorthodox and unheard-of suggestions for treatment, and so, also, these treatments might be considered prophetic.

There are many uses for the laser, as all are aware. Scientists—including Edgar Evans Cayce, Edgar Cayce's second son—understand this to be the same instrument described in the readings as "The Great Crystal," which the Atlanteans used for many purposes. While this could be used for destructive purposes such as "death rays," it could also be used for healing and regenerating the body. In the A.R.E. *Journal,* July, 1967, is the following: "An article entitled 'Laser—the Light Fantastic' by Thomas Meloy in the April, 1967 *Reader's Digest* tells of the recent development of this device, which emits beams of light so intensely concentrated that they can pierce steel. Many uses and possible uses are discussed, including adaptation for surgery. Already eye surgeons are using the laser photocoagulator to repair torn retinas and so ward off detached retinas and resulting blindness. In the laser laboratories of the University of Cincinnati and Children's Hospital in Cincinnati, Dr. Leon Goldman is experimenting with burning off from the skin, blemishes and tumors of a certain kind. Melanomas or cancerous black splotches have turned to healthy white skin tissue in areas touched by the laser beams."

The Cayce readings state: "About the first one (the Great Crystal) . . . It would be well that there be given something of a description of this, that it may be understood . . . how both constructive and destructive forces were generated by the activity of this stone. . . .

"The concentration through the prisms or glass . . . was in such manner that it acted upon the instruments that were connected with the various modes of travel . . . Through the same form of fire the bodies of individuals were regenerated, by the burning—through the application of the rays from the stone, the influence that brought destructive forces to an animal organism. Hence the body rejuvenated itself often. . . ."

The glands, which had been greatly ignored in medical research, have in the past several years become recognized as important in our immunization against bacteria and viruses. This is *not* new, in the Cayce story, for he had much to say about the glands and their function. He said that every organ in the body, in fact, might be termed a gland, but that there are seven centers, or glands, which work together in a healthy body in an intricate way.

In answer to the question, "What relations do the vitamins bear to the glands? Give specific vitamins affecting specific glands," Cayce replied:

"You want a book written on these! They, the vitamins, are food for same. Vitamins are that from which the glands take those necessary influences to supply the energies to enable the varied organs of the body to reproduce themselves. Would it ever be considered that your toenails would be reproduced by the same gland as would supply the breast, the head, or the face? Or that the cuticle would be supplied from the same source as would supply the organ of the heart itself? These [building substances] are taken from glands that control the assimilated foods, and hence require the necessary elements or vitamins in same to supply the various forces for enabling each organ, each functioning of the body, to carry on its creative or generative forces, see?"

Researchers at Wayne State University in Detroit found in 1966 that globulin from a rabbit linked by an organic chemical to cancer cells from a patient, when injected back into the same patient caused antibodies to be developed in his body to fight the cancer!

But back in 1926, a man suffering from cancer was

prescribed a highly predictive treatment, for it was that he be injected with the same kind of rabbit serum! "There may be prepared a serum from the infusion from the pus of this body injected into the rabbit," said Cayce," between the shoulders, and when this brings the infection, this injected or placed on the sore will heal, see? or the culture of same may be made and injected in the blood of this body."

Technological Predictions
Infrasound

The chic secretary in the French National Center for Scientific Research in Marseilles rested her head on her desk. She felt sick, and her pale face looked it.

Soon others on the staff complained. They were nauseated and held their heads in pain. The aspirin bottle was passed around.

What had started as a fine spring day had become a nightmare in which everyone in the building was seized by a mysterious malady.

Investigations revealed that it was not electromagnetic waves, nor was it ultrasound waves, which the laboratory had been researching for eighteen years.

"At this point" states a report special to the *Virginian Pilot*, April 28, 1967, "one of the technicians got out an antique apparatus for detecting infrasound; that is, air vibrations which oscillate at less than ten vibrations a second, or 10 hertz. (The human ear registers, as sound, vibrations from 16 per second, or 16 hertz, to 20,000 hertz.)

"It quickly identified the source of the unease: the giant ventilator of the factory next door. After changing the ventilator's frequency, the five-man team, headed by Prof. Vladimir Gavreau, decided to find out more about the properties of infrasound."

The article goes on to say that "fast sound vibrations go through or bounce off solid objects, usually doing relatively little harm even when very powerful. But slow air vibrations, below the hearing level, can create a sort of pendulum action, a reverberation in solid objects that quickly builds up to intolerable intensity."

To study this phenomenon, the team built a giant whistle

151

and hooked it to a compressed air hose. Then they turned on the air.

"That first test nearly cost us all our lives," Professor Gavreau says. "Luckily, we were able to turn it off fast. All of us were sick for hours. Everything in us was vibrating—stomach, heart, lungs. All the people in the other laboratories were sick. They were very angry with us."

This vibration caused "an irritation so intense that for hours afterwards any low-pitched sound seems to echo through one's body."

"In developing a military weapon, the scientists intend to revert to the policeman's whistle form, perhaps as big as eighteen feet across, mount it on a truck, and blow it with a fan turned by a small airplane engine. It could kill a man five miles away.

"There is one snag. At present, the machine is as dangerous to its operators as it is to the enemy."

This use of "infrasound" to destroy or sicken the enemy seems to have been what was meant by a reading Edgar Cayce gave on September 10, 1936, for Muzuen of Taoi, in the Gobi Desert, 10,000 B.C.:

"As to the manner of defense and offense, as has been indicated, much that is yet to be found again was a part of those preparations in those periods. For these . . . had to do with the setting of long period [slow frequency?] drums for defense in which there might be any attempts by others to interfere, to cause their own undoing."

Whether produced by a whistle or a drum, infrasound seems to be extremely effective!

Electromagnetic Power

The "submarine" looked like a child's toy—only ten feet long, approximately eighteen inches in diameter, it weighed only nine hundred pounds. It was pretty, sleek, white, and of course, unmanned. It had no propellers or jets!

The group of engineers, including senior mechanical engineering students from the University of California at Santa Barbara, who had helped to construct the craft, slowly set it down in the ocean at Guleta by means of hoists. The model was launched and after final balance adjustment, the switch was closed and acceleration began immediately. It moved through the water "at better than design speed" or at 1.5 knots, according to a report by S. Way, consultant for Westinghouse Electric Corporation Research and Development Center.

Now the submarine ploughed along parallel to the shore, turned, came back, and then circled for about twelve minutes. Then it was hauled in and given an inspection and battery check.

And that's how was launched on July 21, 1966, the world's first submarine—since Atlantis, anyway—powered by "those forces in nature as make for iron to swim."

Or, as science has discovered, by electromagnetic forces.

This type of sub could operate just as well in large sizes, says Mr. Way. Such a craft might be considered as an effective cargo carrier.

But the story of the electromagnetic submarine actually started some years ago, when "there was an awakening of interest in the idea of electromagnetic propulsion *in about the year 1958*." (Author's italics.)

So?

"How was this particular Great Pyramid of Gizeh built?" was asked, we will recall, in 1932.

"By the use of those forces in nature as make for iron to swim," said Cayce. "Stone floats in the air in the same manner. This will be discovered in 1958."

A preliminary memorandum on the subject describing Mr. Way's own examination of electromagnetic propulsion was sent to our geologist friend, who relayed his whole story to us. It was dated October 15, 1958! And this was, he stated, its beginning—when memoranda and seminars were presented at the Westinghouse Laboratories dealing with this kind of submarine propulsion.

Hydroelectric Power

The suggestion in 1926 to set up at Bimini a hydroelectric power plant "in the waves . . . by the tides, such as built in the Bay of Fundy" has gone untried. But in 1967 has come the report that a lighthouse in Tokyo Bay has been successfully operated by electricity generated by wave action.

This is Hikajima Lighthouse, and the operation was for a trial thirty day period. The lighthouse, unmanned, is perched on a ledge of rock in the rough surf. The waves flow in, creating air pressure in the tube which is carried through the pipe to an air turbine generator that charges the batteries which operate the light.

The Japanese intend to build a number of these if this one continues operable.

Laser-Operated Space Ship?

On July 2, 1966, *Nature* Magazine carried an article by Professor G. Marx on the possiblity some day of space travel powered by laser beams! The author says it would solve the problem of speed, but slowing down the vehicle upon landing on another planet would be difficult—unless we could radio the planet to let them know we were on the way! Then, after traveling at 0-99c among the stars, the ship could be slowed down by the planet toward which it was headed. The home journey could be made in the same way.

Professor Marx suggests that the difficulty in landing without Earth's technological cooperation probably explains why we haven't been invaded by extraterrestrials so far.

Cayce definitely reported Atlantean travel in craft that "soared through the ether." One such reference was for a man who in 1927 said that at various times during the past six years he had dreamed of an airship heavier than air, which collected its lifting and driving force from the atmosphere by means of *points* on top of it.

"Underneath this machine there are apparently two heavy copper bars running the length of it, having small points underneath which, when charged with the force, lifts the machine from the air, apparently neutralizing the force of gravity.

"The machine was driven by the power streaming from points attached to the rear.

"You will give the interpretation of this dream or vision, tell us if such a machine is practical, and if such a power is available, and how such may be made . . ."

154

Cayce told him that this was "emblematical" of the "higher forces" for spiritual, mental, and physical development. He would have the same dream three more times.

Then Cayce interpreted the dream on a material level, and said that "from the purely mechanical forces, these, as they are presented from time to time, will bring to the knowledge of this man that necessary to bring about the changes in mechanical appliance of that force known as the 'earth side' force as has been applied in eons ago to those crafts that soared through the ether."

Sound like a flying saucer? We think it does! This was twenty years before the first publicized reports of such things, and air travel was in its infancy.

Air Travel

In 1936, you traveled around "upstairs" in dirigibles. You could go to Europe and back that way, although planes were available. But for a number of years, air travel was very unsafe. "Barnstormers" accounted for the high statistics in fatalities, and accidents in general were numerous.

But Edgar Cayce predicted a brighter picture for air travel, and told one traveler: "Regular air travel will become more and more safe. More and more are . . . the airways to become the use of man. . . ."

"Air transportation will become more and more the basis of all relationships with other nations, countries, as well as the internal or national activity," he told another.

"No town or city or community off an airline will be in the thick of things," was another prediction in 1944. "It might as well be out of the world, almost!"

Thus Cayce recognized today's jet age. Today, it's safer to go by air than to drive an automobile. All kinds of safety equipment and safety practices have been provided to cut the hazards.

And although airlines have replaced train travel to a great degree, the railroads are still with us. Cayce had a word to say about that, too: "Railroads will never be entirely eliminated."

Importance of Radio

Although the air was to be the greater means of communication between nations, Cayce said then that radio and telegraph would both be developed as important fields, and that they "must eventually be one." In 1943 he said, "this radio field has only begun to occupy its place in the affairs of men. . . "

He was right. Radio in the form of television, which uses the radio sound system, is with us in a big way. Radio is used now in radio astronomy, in air travel, police communications, and still retains its usefulness as a medium of entertainment.

Electrolysis of Metals

To a man who had in an Egyptian incarnation worked with metals, he said, "Do not give up those ideas of some day experimenting—or this will bear fruition, and you will see it come to pass!"

"What specific experimental work should be done now?" the man asked.

"The combining of the metals in their crude state by the passing of current in the various forms through same, during the period of smelting same, see?" He added, "Copper and brass, gold and iron, through the combinations in their crude state, may be made to be much stronger in usage, lighter in the needs for present development, and not as expensive in the combinations."

The man to see about these possibilities would be Henry Ford, Cayce advised, "if he was approached right."

Electrochemistry has enabled modern industry to make use of this idea but whether or not Henry Ford was approached, in a right or a wrong way, was not given in the record!

Glass That Bends

And then, there was the prediction that it would be possible to make glass that would bend!

The A.R.E. *Journal*, July, 1967, [in *Science News*, Oct. 22, 1966] reports: "A three-page article on the subject of glass reminds us that it was first created when intensely hot volcanic materials flowed over sandy soil and fused this into a smooth, uncrystallized solid. Later, primitive man constructed glass beads as his first manufactured product. Today the making of glass is approached from many angles so that different kinds may answer the varied needs arising in a technological world. The Corning Glass Works has developed a product which is five times stronger than ordinary glass due to a special chemical treatment known as Chemcor. This glass can be bent and twisted without breaking and is especially useful for back windows of sports cars. The Pittsburgh Plate Glass Co. has evolved a method by which chemical tempering replaces heating and quenching. An ion exchange takes place in the glass, bringing greater strength. It can be made very thin and even bent around corners to give streamlined effects without impairment of its toughness."

From the Edgar Cayce readings, the *"World News Spotlight"* report continues: "April 13, 1926. As to what as may be applied in malleable, or in glass that will bend, as is seen and known, the same manner, the same way, of making glass . . . from the elements of the earth's storehouse, is in all practical applications the same as was used twenty-five hundred—yes, forty-five hundred years ago . . . yet there may be still applied those physical elements, now known to man's consciousness, to produce such an element that will act in the place of . . . glass. This, too, however, necessitates the more perfect consciousness of those elements that go to make up flexibility of that called hardened or crystallized substances; for . . . there is no element in the physical plane with the present elasticity of that called glass—that is, a piece, strip of glass, bent in a manner, after becoming crystallized, bended to that point of not breaking, but of its own flexibility, no matter how long same may be kept in that position, the moment it is released, it retains the first or former place or condition. No other element will do such. Hence, as there is seen then, necessary that a greater consciousness of that called crystallization of substances as are known in the make of glass, be gained; though, with study, with a higher concept, a more perfect concept of same, this may become possible."

Remember the glass houses in Edgar Cayce's dream of

the twenty-first century? Do you suppose this will be the natural development from this new discovery? Very likely!

It is not possible here to review all the scientific developments in the Cayce files without a thorough knowledge of science. The many uses now being found for the laser, for instance, were foreshadowed in the Atlantean device, the "firestone" or Great Crystal, which we described in "Atlantis Rising?"

Healing Sound

That infrasound has the power to kill has been demonstrated. But sound has its happier use, as well.

Just as the laser may be used for destruction or for healing, so, too, can sound. It is the low-frequency vibrations which are destructive and which, when produced by an instrument, can kill a man five miles away.

But Cayce had much to say in other readings concerning the use of healing vibrations for people who are both physically and mentally ill, and even for deafness!

Certain kinds of music are more desirable for healing than others. Cayce told several deaf persons, including a child, to listen to music, even though they might not hear it. How would it help? By the vibrations. Such persons should even be encouraged to play an instrument, so as to be healed by the music's resonance.

The most helpful kind of music he said, would be Mendelssohn's "Spring Song," "The Blue Danube," and similar classical and light airs.

"Have you considered the great artist as a pianist who accomplished his greater works when little or no hearing was available of a physical nature?" Cayce reminded one suffering from deafness. "As to how the inner sense was attuned to the infinite?" This, of course, was Beethoven.

Today, many doctors' offices have music piped in to soothe their patients, and music is, in fact, heard in more and more commercial places, including supermarkets, to soothe the customers' pocketbooks!

XIII

THE PRISM TURNS

Edgar Cayce did not try to convince anyone about God, or to set up a cult. Members of the Association have realized this and tried to show that the A.R.E. was a "research organization" rather than a religion. And yet, many people think of it as a form of religion.

This is because many religious ideas have come out of the readings, and are couched in the context of Christian principles. What has emerged has been a much broader understanding of what Christianity is: that although *not* at variance with other religions, it is, after all, the ideal, the most complete faith and the one which is the future religion for the world.

It seems a paradox that the readings present Christianity in this way, until we see what they have to say regarding our relationship to God, and what evolution is all about. Thinking in these terms, considering evolution's span over ages of time, and trying to imagine what we will be like eons from now, the differences between religions seem to dwindle.

"So we see that the coming into earth is—and has ever been—for the soul's evolution," said Cayce, "unto its awareness that there are effects of all influences, in all its experiences, in all its varied spheres of activity. Yet only in Him, the creator and maker who experienced mortality, spirit, and soul, could all this be overcome. For has it not been said and shown . . . that He has not willed any should be lost?"

He went on to say that His Spirit has been in the leaders of all religions and "in every race and color." In another reading he states that the Christ "as an entity influenced

159

either directly or indirectly all those forms of philosophy or religious thought that taught God was One" such as "Buddhism, Muhammedanism, Confucianism, Shintoism, Brahmanism, Platonism, Judaism."

Religion in the Cayce records cannot be confined to limited boundaries. It runs throughout every reading, whether physical, mental, or spiritual, whether on science or sociology, for all ages, for people of all faiths. There is an underlying truth which is consistent, and which cuts across all manmade lines.

In 1931, Cayce predicted that one woman would live to see "the greatest development in spiritual affairs that the world has known." In the thirty-seven years since that time, has the world developed spiritually? Memories of personal experience and of what has happened to the world during that time would probably make most people answer *No!* After all these years, on the eve of upheavals in the earth we don't quite believe will be possible, and amid the very real upheavals going on in our cities and among the best and the worst of us, the answer seems to be the slogan "God is dead!"

But even science is not quite convinced of this idea, as Dr. A.K. Reischauer points out in *"The Nature and Truth of the Great Religions.* He states: "The older materialistic and mechanistic cosmologies are no longer intellectually respectable. To be sure, the concept of mechanism will continue to function for certain aspects of the physical cosmos, but to accept it as adequate for reality on all its levels or for reality as a whole is regarded as naively childish."

"Mind is the Builder," said Cayce many times, explaining how a life, a concept, a nation, a world is created. Never did he say that the universe is a mechanical toy operating mindlessly and without the concern of a Creator out there!

Dr. Reischauer quotes a passage from *The Mysterious Universe* by Sir James H. Jeans, one of the greatest astronomers and physicists of modern times, that confirms what Cayce has said all along about the Mind of the Universe: "Today there is a wide measure of agreement, which on the physical side of science approaches almost to unanimity, that the stream of knowledge is leading towards a non-mechanical reality; the universe begins to look more like a great thought than like a great machine. Mind no longer appears as an accidental intruder into the realm of matter; we are beginning to suspect that we ought rather to hail it as the creator and governor of the realm of matter. . . .

"The new knowledge compels us to revive our hasty first impressions that we had stumbled into a universe which either did not concern itself with life or was entirely hostile to life. The old dualism of mind and matter, which was mainly responsible for the supposed hostility, seems likely to disappear; not through matter becoming in any way more shadowy or insubstantial than heretofore, or through mind becoming resolved into a function of the working of matter, but through substantial matter resolving itself into a creation and manifestation of mind. We discover that the universe shows evidence of a designing or controlling power that has something in common with our own individual minds—not: so far as we have discovered, emotion, morality, or aesthetic appreciation, but the tendency to think in the way which, for want of a better word, we describe as Mathematical. . . .

"It is, in fact, most striking," Dr. Reischauer continues, "how many modern scientists and philosophers give recognition to the mental and spiritual aspect of the physical cosmos. It is as Eddington puts it when he says rather whimsically, 'There *is* an external world . . . But I think there can be no doubt that the scientist has a much more mystical conception of the external world than he had in the last century where every scientific "explanation" of phenomena proceeded on the assumption that nothing could be true unless an engineer could make a model of it.' "

This kind of thinking is bound to filter down from the Olympian heights to the common man! Thus, the old materialism seems to be giving way to a fulfillment of Cayce's prophecy of "the greatest development in spiritual affairs the world has ever known."

The reforms that have been going on, both in the Roman Catholic Church and in the Protestant churches, as the result of self-criticism and a general reassessment of their role in today's changing world, is another part of the prophecy come true. Who can say fully what is going on in the spiritual world, or who is the final authority? We observe these movements from a limited vantage point, and do not attempt to evaluate their meaning. We can only point out what seems to have been meant by Cayce's prediction.

At a time in which every churchgoer, every college and high school student, is dismayed and intimidated by the conflict between science and religion that still is felt, crippling the layman's ability to accept the Bible's great truth, and yet undermining our understanding of what science's ultimate gift to mankind is, we are refreshed by such statements made by scientists for the general masses as acknowledge the existence of God.

Such a statement is the following by Dr. Wernher von Braun, director of NASA's Marshall Space Flight Center in Huntsville, Ala., from an article in the *Tampa Tribune,* July 30, 1966 (quoted by permission of the North American Newspaper Alliance): "The two most powerful forces shaping our civilization today are science and religion. Through science, man strives to learn more of the mysteries of creation. Through religion, he seeks to know the Creator.

"Neither operates independently. It is as difficult for me to understand a scientist who does not acknowledge the presence of a superior rationality behind the existence of the universe as it is to comprehend a theologian who would deny the advances of science. . . .

"Today, thousands of scientists all over the world are engaged in the greatest intellectul adventure ever undertaken by man: Attempting to understand the origin and functioning of a physical universe that is vast in space and time, complicated in detail, and awesome in its orderliness.

"Thus, to say that science's only purpose is trying to discover physical laws to increase man's control over the forces of nature is no longer an adequate explanation of science's goal; for the concept of science itself has grown. The raw material of science is a set of experiences, observations, and measurements with which the scientist attempts to build a model of time, space, and matter. When new knowledge is discovered, the old model is not discarded; it is simply changed according to the pattern of relationships which the scientist finds in this set of experiences.

"By his willingness to change his model or his concepts,

the scientist is admitting that he makes no claim to possessing ultimate truth.

"You cannot build a wall between science and religion. As science explains more of the intriguing mysteries of life and the universe, its realms expand into those areas which previously were either unknown or accepted solely by faith. Every experience we have—physical or spiritual—must fit together into a pattern that is credible and meaningful. Man is the observer of the universe, the experimenter, the searcher for truth, but he is not a spectator alone. He is a participant in the continuing process of creation. . . .

"In our modern world many people seem to feel that our rapid advances in the field of science render such things as religious beliefs untimely or old-fashioned. They wonder why we should be satisfied in 'believing' something when science tells us that we 'know' so many things. The simple answer to this contention is that we know many more mysteries of nature today than when the Age of Scientific Enlightenment began. There is certainly no scientific reason why God cannot retain the same position in our modern world that He held before we began probing His creation with telescope and cyclotron. . . .

"Our decisions undeniably influence the course of future events. Nature around us still harbors more unsolved than solved mysteries. But science has mastered enough of these forces to usher in a golden age for all mankind if this power is used for good—or to destroy us if evil triumphs. The ethical guidelines of religion are the bonds that can hold our civilization together. Without them man can never attain that cherished goal of lasting peace with himself, his God, and his fellow man."

As has been observed, religion is not confined to a special category in the Cayce readings and is hard to separate from the general picture of his prophecies. We have already pointed out that the spirtuality of the American people would be the criterion for the peace of the world. We have had the shocking prediction that "out of Russia's religious development would come the hope of the world." We have the amazing forecast that China will one day be the "cradle of Christianity."

These, given in the chapter "Destiny of Nations," emphasize that the spirituality of a people shapes their destiny. It was the loss of religious ideals, we recall, which brought about the Atlantean catastrophe. Then to what religious thought will the world turn in the days ahead, to shape its future?

"That as is comprised in that as has been given, whether it be the Greek or the barbarian, whether it be from the bond or from the free, 'Thou shalt love the Lord thy God with all thine heart, and thy neighbor as thyself!' " said Cayce.

He stressed that religion was not a matter of belonging to a church but that "the church is within self." He advised that one should join a church, not for convenience, but "where ye may serve the better."

This understanding as to what true worship is was given us in John 4: 19-26: "The woman said to him, 'Sir, I perceive that you are a prophet. Our fathers worshiped on this mountain; and you say that in Jerusalem is the place where men ought to worship.' Jesus said to her, 'Woman, believe me, the hour is coming when neither on this mountain nor in Jerusalem will you worship the Father. You worship what you do not know; we worship what we know, for salvation is from the Jews. But the hour is coming, and now is, when the true worshipers will worship the Father in spirit and truth, for such the Father seeks to worship Him. God is spirit, and those who worship him must worship in spirit and truth.' The woman said to him, 'I know that Messiah is coming (he who is called Christ); when he comes, he will show us all things.' Jesus said to her, 'I who speak to you am he.' "

Someone asked Cayce, "Is there any indication of what church I should join and associate with?"

"Remember, rather, the church is within self," he answered. "As to the organization, choose that, not as a convenience for thee but where ye may serve the better . . . whatever its name, let it be thy life proclaiming Jesus the Christ."

"For the Master built no churches, but He laid the foundations." He told another person that the church was within, as he had learned in a former incarnation: "Before that, the entity was in the English land during those periods when questioning arose between church and state. And there the entity for itself settled that question for good: the church is within yourself and not in any pope or preacher, or in any building, but in self. For thy body is indeed the temple of the living God and the Christ becomes a personal companion in mind and in body. . ."

Individual preferences and temperaments should be considered, Cayce said, in choosing one's church. "Then let each test themselves with that chosen. That it will make for life in thine own experience will aid another. Not that each has the same vision, or the same experience, but the Lord addeth to the church daily such as should be saved, when all of one mind!"

Cayce interpreted Jesus' prophecy: "Upon this I will build my church." "What church? The Holy Church! Who is the head? That One upon whom the conditions had been set by that question asked. For here ye may find the answer again to many of those questions sought concerning the Spirit, the Church, the Holy Force that manifests by the attuning of the individual; though it may be for a moment.

"He asked, 'Whom say men that I am?' Then Peter answered, 'Thou art the Christ, the son of the living God!' Then, 'Upon this I will build my church and the gates of hell shall not prevail against it!'

"The New Jerusalem"

"In Revelation 21, what is the meaning of the new heaven and the new earth; for the first heaven and the first earth were passed away and there were no more seas?"

This question was answered by Cayce as follows: "When the foundations of the earth are broken up by those very disturbances. Can the mind of man comprehend no desire of sin, no purpose but that the glory of the Son may be manifested in his life? Is this not a new heaven, a new earth? For the former things would have passed away. For as the desires, the purposes, the aims are to bring about the whole change physically, so does it create in the experience of each soul a new vision, a new comprehension.

"For, as has been given, it hath not entered the heart of

man to know the glories that have been prepared, that are a part of the experiences of those that love only the Lord and His ways."

We recall that Jerusalem was the place of the Temple rebuilt for the Jews by Herod, where for two thousand years before Christ's Advent, the Jews had worshipped. Jerusalem has long been an important city to the nations, and to the Christians, Jews, Moslems, it has held a special significance.

An explanation of the following verse was then asked of Cayce: "And I saw the holy city, new Jerusalem, coming down out of heaven from God, prepared as a bride adorned for her husband; and I heard a great voice from the throne saying, 'Behold, the dwelling of God is with men. He will dwell with them, and they shall be his people, and God Himself will be with them: He will wipe away every tear from their eyes, and death shall be no more, neither shall there be mourning nor crying nor pain any more, for the former things are passed away." (Rev. 21:4)

Cayce explained, "[To] those then, that are come into the new life, the new understanding—the new regeneration, there *is* then the new Jerusalem—not as a place, alone, but as a condition, as an experience of the soul.

"Jerusalem has figuratively, symbolically, meant the holy place, the Holy City, for there the Ark of the Covenant—in the minds, the hearts, the understandings, the comprehensions of those who have put away the earthly desires and become as the *new* purposes in their experience, become the New Jerusalem, the new undertakings, the new desires."

Here we find echoed what Cayce described for the conditions of the New Age, and that it is both of the future, and, for those who are truly one with God's purpose, *now*. Jesus told the Samaritan woman that "the hour is coming, and now is, when the true worshippers will worship the Father in spirit and truth." Even then, the New Age had begun, and the New Jerusalem was present!

We remember that Cayce said that during this age many high-minded individuals are being incarnated on earth to assist in its culmination. Cayce was asked to explain this admonition: "Do not seal up the words of the prophecy of this book, for the time is near. Let the evildoer still do evil, and the filthy still be filthy, and the righteous still do right, and the holy still be holy. (Rev. 22: 10-11)

Cayce's interpretation: "As that period approaches when there shall be the influences of the power of those incarnated in the activities of the earth, then the purposes become set as in that indicated by the activities of each being in that to which they have then given themselves."

That we can use power either for good or for destruction is by now a familiar statement of the nature of man's full abilities. So great is man's power of free will, said Cayce, that he literally doesn't know his own strength!

This idea appears in a reading given in 1935. Cayce was asked, "Regarding general world conditions, is it likely that changes in the earth's surface in the Mediterranean area will stop Italy's campaign against Ethiopia?"

"Not at this particular period," was the answer. "Such changes may eventually be part of the earth's experience, but not just yet."

"When is this likely to occur?"

"As to times and places and seasons—as indeed has been indicated in the greater relationshps established by prophets and sages of old—especially as given by Him: 'As to the day and hour, who knoweth? No, one, save the Creative Forces.'

"Tendencies in the hearts and souls of men are such that these upheavals may be brought about. For as often indicated through these channels: Man is not ruled by the world, the earth, the environs about it, nor the planetary influences with their associations and activities. Rather it is true that man brings order out of chaos by his compliance with Divine Law. Or by his disregard of the laws of Divine influence, man brings chaos and destructive forces into his experience.

"For He hath given: 'Though the heavens and the earth pass away, my word shall not pass away.' This is often considered just a beautiful saying, or a thought to awe those who have been stirred by some experience. But let us apply these words to conditions existent in the affairs of the world and the universe at present. What holds them together—what are the foundations of the earth? The word of the Lord!"

In *The Dawn of Conscience* (New York: Scribners,

1933) James H. Breasted gives us an insight strangely parallel to the Cayce view of history and how man shapes it. At the time his book appeared, the world was still thinking in the old ways, so that his thoughts are all the more remarkable for their timeliness now. In his final chapter, "Power and Character," he says: "In Palestine this is indeed the supreme transformation, from Elijah to Jesus, from Carmel and Armageddon to Nazareth.

"But this culmination in Palestine was a later process, a fruition made possible by that far earlier transformation—what we have called the great transformation—which lifted man from the exclusive struggle with nature alone and shifted him into a new arena, the struggle with *himself* for the conquest of his own soul and those new values which transcend the material world and make up the substance of a new reality which we call character. We have seen that the forces which wrought this earlier transformation were born in Egypt and passed thence to Palestine and the later world. It was no merely accidental coincidence that Hebrew history should have traced Hebrew national origins back to Egypt, a tradition of which there is an echo in the Christian belief, 'Out of Egypt have I called my son.'

"Today in the lands of the ancient East we too look out upon the works of nature and the works of man, and in a New Crusade of scientific endeavor, we are striving to recover the story of both. But already we have discerned enough to realize that they are *one:* that the processes of nature and the unfolding life of man are but chapters of the same great story; that looking down into that appalling chasm of the Dead Sea which so terribly confronts us with Professor Haeckel's question (Is the universe friendly?), we may find an answer which natural science cannot give us—an answer which comes to us only as we contemplate human experience in the Ancient East and realize that the culmination of a developing universe is *character.*

"It has been the purpose of this book to furnish an historical demonstration that the process of human advance which brought forth character is still unfinished—is still going on. The possibilities of its future are *unlimited,* and it is our responsibility to bring the vast significance of this new fact to bear as a practical influence upon our own conduct. In doing so we gain the full realization that we are no longer carrying forward merely traditional truths and inherited teachings with which we may have little sympathy, but just as the light of character once dawned in a darkness which had never known such light before, so there is no reason to doubt the growth of that light to illumine realms of being that still lie all unrealized in the unfathomed ages toward which our limited vision of today looks out but does not see."

In November, 1932, the physical changes predicted in Alabama for 1936-38 were on the mind of one person, and Cayce's answer to the question "What form will they take?" was also the answer to a much larger question, for it pointed to the idea that man's character and the processes of nature are, in Breasted's words, "but chapters of the same great story."

"To be sure," said Cayce, "that may depend upon much that deals with metaphysical as well as what people call actual, or in truth! For as understood—or should be understood by the entity—there are those conditions that in the activity of individuals, in line of thought and endeavor, oft keep many a city and many a land intact, through their application of the spiritual laws in their associations with individuals. This will take more of the form here in the change, as we find, through the sinking of portions, with the following up of the inundations by this overflow.

"In all these times, let each declare whom ye will serve: A nation, a man, a state, or thy God?"

XIV

EVOLUTION: IT'S WHAT'S HAPPENING!

Three-year-old Belinda Le Blanc crept softly behind her mother's chair and said in an awesome treble: "Ooooh! I'm a ghooost!"

Silence. Mother looked back of her chair. "Ooooh! I'm a bigger ghost than youooo!"

Belinda shrieked with delight.

It was December, 1932, and her mother sought a reading for Belinda from Edgar Cayce.

Belinda was, said her reading, talented in music, and one who loved mysteries. "Coming under the influence of Neptune makes for mystic forces . . . in making a mystery, in soft whispers, in creeping about. . . .

"This may be enhanced or entirely eliminated by the trend of the development."

But Belinda poses a lesson for all those interested in training and teaching unusual children, in developing a better society, in helping to work out man's destiny. For she was first described as a very "old soul" who would be "unusual."

Her reading volunteered the prediction that man would come to understand an important fact—that the development of the human mind will represent the development of the human race not through biological, but through sociological conditions in man's progress or evolution.

An old soul, such as Belinda, then, was "the more highly evolved" or "greater developed soul" because, Cayce said, she had lived a great period of time in history.

There are old souls and there are young souls. Some of us have grown spiritually, others have regressed. Some have many experiences on earth to their credit; others, few.

170

But it has been according to the will of the individual, not God's. We call to mind Cayce's statement that "all those who have forgotten God have gradually been eliminated," and that only souls that have reached a certain level of development (for to remember God must be the requirement) have been permitted to incarnate.

There is a place for all of us in the great Heart of the Universe. It is, however, given us to know that it is a special privilege to incarnate, and that many souls crowd about the earth, seeking an opportunity for rebirth.

But from the above, we infer that for this age, the standards are higher and the restrictions more stringent. As we have come along, throughout many lives, we have matured in soul attributes and gradually the human race has gotten better.

A New Step in Man's Understanding

Evolution, we said in the chapter on the religion of the future, was for the soul's growth: "Coming into earth has been for the soul's evolution."

There is a double prediction given in the Cayce record that we almost overlooked, it was so mildly put. And yet, to me it seems quite a special kind of prediction. It was given for little Belinda and it related to her because she was an old soul. Cayce seemed to be prompted by some soul records to call up the most amazing observations! This was one.

It dealt with the workings of reincarnation as being for the soul's evolution: "As may be well understood (and will become gradually more and more understood by the mental-mind of man), the developing of the mental attributes of the human family will grow more and more to represent the whole period of transition, in the way of developing the human race of family through that known as the form, not of biological, but of sociological, conditions in the evolution of man in each experience (or incarnation)."

To paraphrase, he is saying that (1) the developing of human mental attributes will in the future represent, not biological evolution, but sociological; and (2) the mind of man will gradually understand this new concept.

A *third* prediction is implied: that man will accept rein-carnation as a fact, because this is necessary in order to accept the first!

What would sociological evolution be? That Breasted referred to in his *Dawn of Conscience*, in which man is pictured developing a social consciousness and character based on his humanitarian insights. Not that man *inherited* his character and his nobler instincts, so much as learned them from the examples of a few good, upstanding citizens, and taught them to his children.

At least, that is what is meant generally to distinguish from biological evolution, in which survival of the fittest has been the teacher.

But Cayce added, "in each experience (or incarnation)," thus including the factor of reincarnation. So the sociological evolution he predicted must be understood to be accomplished by man learning to do better through his own personal soul growth, rather than the hand-me-down methods we have thought were sufficient.

For the rebirth experience is, according to reincarnationists, much more effective for teaching the lessons of soul growth than any teacher or text!

Or, to put it another way: The science teacher can talk all he wants about a theory, but it's in the laboratory where the student experiences the realities of that theory.

When Cayce gave this prediction, science was closer to the Darwinian theory of evolution, and the widespread misconceptions concerning his *Origin of Species*. The public thought he had said that man came from monkeys, whereas he had avoided man's evolution in the book.

But Cayce reflected the *future* thinking in his readings on evolution, and anticipated science's modern and enlightened stand on theory that man came from monkeys: by disagreeing.

"Archeology has made great strides in the century since Darwin set the world agog," writes Dr. Webb B. Garrison, author of *Strange Bonds Between Animals and Men*. "Mounting numbers of finds in Africa and Asia, as well as in Europe, have clarified the evolutionary paths of both men and apes. Today, no serious scientist supports the notion that humans are descendants of living anthropoid species—to say nothing of the long-popular view that Negroes

172

sprang from gorillas, Mongolians from orangs, and whites from chimpanzees!

"New fossil finds plus more accurate dating by means of radiocarbon and other recent techniques have given conclusive proof that man is far older than any Victorian dared guess. Peking man, one of several human species long extinct, seems to have been using bone tools and fire some 400,000 to 600,000 years ago. Even Neanderthal man, whose skullcap was ammunition for Huxley's assault upon the taken-for-granted, is no longer considered to have been a direct ancestor of *Homo sapiens.*

"Most specialists now think that modern man, several extinct groups, and today's great apes are descendants from an unknown type of primate that thrived at least 30,000,000 years ago. Vague and scattered clues suggest that the family tree branched some 25,000,000 years ago. One line is thought to have produced the gibbon, while the other is believed to have continued toward human and ape types.

"At least half a million years ago—and probably much earlier—still obscure genetic changes led to the appearance of *Homo erectus.* . . .

"Long extinct, this early human was followed by big-brained *Homo sapiens,* to which species belong all the varied races of men. . . ."

Cayce's interpretation of evolution holds that man evolved biologically but that this has always been that his "flesh . . . was always to meet the needs of man for which there was made all that was made." He added that our evolving has been "the gradual growth upward to the mind of the Maker."

Instead, however, of evolving from lower forms of life, we originated from "the First Cause, or God, in creation, and the preparation for our future needs has gone down many, many thousands and millions of years." This is in preparation "for the needs of man in the hundreds of thousands of years to come."

According to Cayce, this is the only inhabited planet in this solar system and all the universe was indeed created for man's evolvement back to God! Our other planets, he said, don't even have animal life of any kind.

173

The predictions here given are in need of fuller explanation and analysis by a more competent mind; I will not attempt to do more than state them. I conclude that Cayce is saying that man is a social being more than a biological being, and that this will be very important to us as we learn more about the mind. He is basically from the "First Cause" which commands him to be a cooperative, peaceful, loving part of a larger Being. He develops *to* this and learns by experience over long periods of time, his character and his mental attributes being shaped by his own trial and error in many lifetimes. He learns, not in a vacuum, but in a universe that is a *social* universe which includes many mysteries—not the least of which is man himself. But he finds within himself all that is in the universe, and all that is finally necessary, and he translates this to his attitudes and his actions toward God and his fellow man.

Forshadowing this predicted change in scientific attitudes toward man's high status in the scheme of things is this statement by Dr. Garrison: "Maturing knowledge has led to a new understanding of the grandeur of the creature who is unique as asker of questions and finder of answers about animals and men."

"It's What's Happening"

Where are we headed? If we have gradually changed and developed for the better, as Cayce says, where do we go from here? Is it possible we could be improved as a race? Yes, said Cayce, that's what's happening! Man is growing up.

Suddenly the world is aware of the powers of the mind, the ability of some people to predict the future, to see colors with their fingers, to practice thought transference. This awakening is everywhere and in many areas of activity. The religious awakening among people both in and out of the church is a part of it, as are the rise of many new scientific ideas and revival in the arts, we believe.

The riots, the violence, the immorality, the minority of our youth who rebel against the traditional good life, are happening, too. The awakening is a two-edged sword and brings with it a negative side to which some are drawn.

But the meaning is there. It is the pervasive, unspoken and yet very real feeling which runs through all of it that man is coming into his own, and that we are being thrust forward toward something better than before.

We have been told, in fact, in the Old and the New Testaments, (Psalms 82; John 10:34), that we are gods! But we're self-made gods, and have to earn the right, on every level, for what we claim.

Cayce predicted that we will develop psychic powers just as we have developed our senses: through long generations of the *need* for such abilities. Just as we acquired eyesight, rather than the sharp hearing of the dolphin, so will we acquire extrasensory perception. Our sight was sharpened because we have an environment of light which makes vision possible. The dolphin, however, has developed in the sea where sound carries, but vision is hampered in the murky depths.

Dare we assume, then, that it will be because we are entering a new environment of the universe in which Earth has never before found itself, as Cayce suggests, where the vibrations are such that we will need psychic ability? If man has developed, as he says, according to biological needs that have been fulfilled to help him grow "upward to the mind of his Maker," then there is no reason to doubt that he will do so according to new needs taking him even closer to that goal.

Cayce stated we would develop intuition and telepathy, and that in fact this has been going on among various cultures over centuries of time. The Bible is perhaps our best guide to this side of man, for both the Old and the New Testaments are actually an account of man's psychic experience, although primarily of the Jewish heritage. Joseph's predictive dreams, the story of the witch of Endor, the visions of the prophets, the early Christians' speaking in tongues, the appearances of angels and cherubim, all this is of the past. But these stories are still told as unusual happenings, as extraordinary then as they would be for us today. So we know that psychic powers have manifested only here and there, and have always been a source of much doubt and speculation.

Cayce defined psychic phenomena with the explanation that "psychic" means "of the Spirit or soul." He added that psychic forces are "of the imagination when attuned to the spirit or the soul of the individual" or they may be from other entities or souls that have passed on. They are real. They are not understood from the physical standpoint, but may be understood by an intuitive, receptive mind.

Without the psychic world, the physical world would be in a state of "hit or miss" or as "a ship without a rudder." It is the *building force* in each and every condition. No healing, for instance, is perfected without some psychic force on the part of a doctor, nurse, or loved one.

Psychic readings such as Cayce gave were given among the Chaldeans four thousand years before Christ. They seemed to be accompanied, said Cayce, by magnetic healing, of "that life-giving flow" of psychic force.

Such readings *should* be given, if not used for selfish reasons, and the use of this force is only "using the spiritual law that makes one free." This does not mean the freedom to take advantage of one's fellowman or to hurt him.

Where did the information given through Edgar Cayce originate? It was, said he, gathered from the sources from which the suggestion (given at the beginning of a reading) may derive its information. His mind communicated with those like minds having to do with the person involved. There is a vast fund of information in the collective unconscious whereupon Cayce drew, mysteriously and unerringly.

Not only will we develop the ability in this Aquarian Age to communicate telepathically, Cayce predicted, but we will have the full consciousness of being able to communicate with the Creative Forces and to make use of them as scientific laws for our material benefit!

This means we will have a kind of "mental radio" which will put us in touch with the universe! But only those who can accept it will even know what's going on.

It is difficult for our practical, scientifically-geared minds to believe what was said here about the future nature of man's mental abilities, and yet the stirrings are evident everywhere around us. Psychics like Peter Hurkos and Gerard Croiset are being employed by police departments to help solve crimes. Scientists are conducting experiments in ESP, life after death, psychic photography, color vision. Universities around the world are granting doctorate degrees for this kind of research, including Yale, Cambridge, and Oxford. Leningrad University has a special department for this.

The novelist Taylor Caldwell has recently revealed in *This Week* magazine (Oct. 15, 1967) that she has the gift of ESP and the ability to predict events. She describes her attempts to be understood for her insights, and the negative reactions which she received. Only now has she broken her long silence regarding her gift, for she feels she has important predictions to make.

It was Jeane Dixon's unique influence in the world today which broke the spell—Jess Stearn and Ruth Montgomery, her biographers, making it possible for such people as Miss Caldwell to speak up to a world turned more sympathetic to people of her unusual abilities. And even for this, Edgar Cayce had a prediction: He foretold that a man by the name of Stearn or "Sterne" would make Cayce's work known in a big way. And he did!

Developing Psychic Abilities

One of Cayce's predictions was phrased in this way: "The individuals of this plane [Earth] will and are developing this [thought transference] as the senses were and are developed."

Some people who came to Cayce for readings were already aware of their advanced mental abilities, and asked questions to explain the phenomena they had encountered. One person asked: "In the physical plane, do the thoughts of another person affect a person either mentally or physically?"

Cayce replied: "Depending upon the development of the individual to whom the thought may be directed."

Apparently, then, we are on various levels of this evolutionary progress. It was in this reading that he volunteered the prediction that this would develop among all of us as a general trend.

Another person who perhaps did not have psychic ability but who was interested in cultivating it asked, "How does one develop psychic powers?"

"The preparation for tomorrow is builded on today," Cayce told her. Those experiences we have now are used

177

for the growth of mental and spiritual attributes of the future. Of course, we can choose not to develop them, just as we can choose to shut off sounds audible to our normal hearing. It is our will which, after all, is paramount in our progress. "That the will must be the ever-guiding factor to lead man on, ever upward" was the understanding to be gained from our study of the planets.

"To him that hath, and uses aright, to him shall be given. To him that hath and abuses that privilege, to him shall be taken away even that he seemed to have," was a statement Cayce made elsewhere. but which seems to apply here. As we use our psychic powers, however slight, we will be given more. But we must really want to do so, to acquire them.

In a sense, Ella Johansen was asking for all of us who might want to be more psychic, when she posed the question: "While in this body will I ever be able to see and hear on a higher plane? How can I develop this power?"

This attunement, Cayce said, is accomplished only in concentration and in attuning oneself to those forces on higher planes. A person is made up of various consciousnesses. As he opens himself to these "various spheres of understanding," he gains "an access, a vision, an insight, a hearing, a feeling, into these various planes." He attains the next plane by using the gifts at hand.

Belief in the psychic sources available to us, as they were to Cayce, can only come with personal experience. There are laws that govern the use of these powers, just as laws govern the use of electricity—and they can be just as dangerous if used wrong! Even Cayce was not able at all times to read the record or the collective mind for a person if the person was unwilling to submit to the suggestion. Sometimes his own ill health hindered. Or perhaps the mental attitude of those about him was not in accord with the kind of information sought.

In one instance, no information at all came through, because of the "feelings of those present that made for a deflecting of that being sought."

"The development must be self-development, soul development."

Thus Cayce advised a young electrical engineering student on "correctly developing psychic faculties." He said that this person was well balanced mentally, physically and spiritually, but that he could use his psychic forces for either very high development or for the turning of it into destructive forces, though not intentionally at all times.

So he was warned, "Find self. Find what is self's ideal. And as to how high that ideal is. Does it consist of or pertain to self development (or selfless development) for the glory of the ideal? And be sure that the ideal is rather of the spiritual. . . .

"And do not be satisfied with a guide other than from the Throne of Grace itself! . . . And who better may be such a guide (to teach him) than the Creator *of* the universe? For, He has given that 'If ye will seek me ye may find me' and 'I will not leave thee comfortless' but if ye are righteous in purpose, in intent, in desire, 'I will bring *all things* to thine remembrance' that are needs be for thy soul, thine mind, thine body, development. . . .

"This is a promise from Him, who is able to fulfill that which has been promised to every soul that seeks His face, His ways.

"Then, speak oft with thy Maker. And let thine meditation be:

"Lord, use thou me in that way, in that manner, that I—as thy son—thy servant—may be of the greater service to my fellow man. And may I know His biddings, Father, as Thou hast promised that if we would hear Him, that we ask in His Name may be ours. I *claim* that relationship, Father, and I seek thy guidance day by day!"

This young man was told that he would receive guidance within, knowing the answers "in the spirit." When some associate, or friend, or brother came along "as a guidepost along the way of life," he would know that he had been guided to that person and "must walk that road," learning what that person could teach him.

The Key to Telepathy

Telepathy seems to be the most common form of ESP and the most easily developed. "Give the principles and techniques of conscious telepathy," one person asked.

"The consciousness of His abiding presence" was the

answer. "For He is all power, all thought, the answer to every question. For, as these attune more and more to the awareness of His presence, the desire to know of those influences that may be revealed caused the awareness to be materially practical.

"First, begin between selves. Set a definite time and each at that moment put down what the other is doing. Do this twenty days. And ye shall find ye have the key to telepathy."

Possession To Be Understood

To accept that there is such a thing as demonic possession is to accept the existence of an invisible spirit world. For this reason, despite Jung's assertion that possession exists, psychology still does not recognize that premise.

However, in giving help for a case which he named possession, Cayce made the prediction that although this interpretation would not be admitted by some as an explanation, "there will come those days when many will understand and interpret properly." Several cases of insanity brought to Cayce for readings turned out to be cases of possession, he said. Such was a young man who would not respond to the usual treatment for schizophrenia, and whose condition was only worsened by sedatives given him.

As man applies the laws of the universe, he develops and brings up the whole generation of man, said Cayce. Individuals carry out certain elements and laws, and gradually man becomes capable of applying and using these in his everyday life. This, whether applied in medical science, anatomical science, mechanical science, or whatever, is merely discovery of universal laws that have ever been existent in the universe.

"Many times has the evolution of the earth reached the stage of development as it has today and then sank again, to rise again the next development—some along one line, some along others: for often we find that the higher branches of so-called learning destroy themselves in the seed they produce in man's development, as we have in medical force, as we have in astrological, spiritual, destructive forces. . . ."

Our example here is, of course, that of Atlantis. The people of that highly developed continent were, said Cayce, a "thought people," with greatly evolved mental and intuitive abilities. They had a better understanding of spiritual laws than we do today; yet they were weakened by the "Sons of Belial"—those who served the dark forces—and were destroyed from within. As we learned from their history in the readings, they had developed on all levels: they were gifted in science and the arts, and possessed the psychic abilities we are just becoming aware of in this age. They had many conveniences—necessities to them, although we would think of them as luxuries. They were able to use ESP to their own advantage, and many of them used it for good. Some men and women were told in the readings that they had been prophets in their own right, and thus would take in stride the many supernatural events that are a part of their experience. For instance, they knew from the prophecies of their leaders that Atlantis was doomed, and were able to prepare well in advance for the breaking up of their civilization. They collected their documents and put them into the Tomb of Records, knowing that centuries might follow without so much as a hint of their having existed, and yet, knowing, too, of the prophecies of this age, when all would be revealed.

The experience of Atlantis, then, is a lesson to this generation in the evolution of the earth, and man's capacity for making a total shambles of his sojourn here. For, says Cayce, not only has this happened to the Atlantean civilization, it has happened to many before it!

"You remember a single deluge only," states the Egyptian priest, in Plato's *Republic*. "There have been, and will be again, many destructions of mankind arising out of many causes. . . . You remember a single deluge, only, but there were many previous ones."

This time, we believe, things will be different.

We must believe it.

XV

TIME AND PROPHECY

How is prophecy possible?

Destiny, said Edgar Cayce, is created in Time and Space.

"Those activities (of men) make for such an impression upon the realm of data, or between Time and Space, as to make for what men have called Destiny . . . in the material affairs of individuals."

Then, we might ask along with J.B. Priestly, author of *Man and Time*,* "What is Time?" Or, as he states it, "What is the future?" For of course the future is a part of time. "The future can be seen, and because it can be seen, it can be changed. But if it can be seen and yet be changed, it is neither solidly there, laid out for us to experience, moment after moment, nor is it non-existent, something we are helping to create, moment after moment. If it does not exist, it cannot be seen; if it is solidly set and fixed, then it cannot be changed. What is this future that is sufficiently established to be observed and perhaps experienced, and yet can allow itself to be altered?"

God, said Cayce, is Time, Space and Patience. And all Time is one: the past, present, and future.

"For to the entity—as to the world—patience is the lesson that each soul must learn in its journey through materiality. And this is a thought for the entity: Time, Space, Patience are in the mental realm the same as implied by the expression "Father-God, Son, and Holy Spirit"; or as Spirit, Body, Soul. They are expressions of the three-dimensional thought. And in Patience then does

*New York: Doubleday, 1964

182

man become more and more aware of the continuity of life, of his soul being a portion of the Whole. . . ."

Time and Space are difficult concepts to grasp. We can take them in limited portions, only. And yet, they do not appear quite so awesome when we realize that they are a part of our everyday lives. The daily, three-dimensional events which we can understand are, after all, events which are a part of Eternity.

For instance, at the time of the Deluge, according to Genesis, people were going about their daily lives pretty much as usual. They were "eating and drinking and marrying" at the very moment disaster overtook them. They obviously didn't know what Time it was!

All that we know in our lives materially is measurable, evaluated in terms of the abstract realities we call time and space. We move around in space without much thought. Sometimes we are forced to be aware of it when we stand on a crowded bus, and sometimes, looking at the stars, we are bowled over by its magnitude. We buy and sell footage in county fairs; we rent it in parking lots. It takes half an acre or more to build a house and plant a tree.

We are conscious as never before, in the history we know, of the galaxies and universes. We find ourselves in a "space race" to control the square mileage out there.

By means of the sun, or a watch, or a Stonehenge, we measure time. We are aware of time in relation to our lives and the events they encompass—or in relation to history and the happenings recounted in their sequence.

Time is precious to us all, but we use it each in his own way, and out of it are shaped individual lifetimes, are they not? Time is not the same to us all, however, nor is it the same to us at all times.

So time and space remain mysteries that bring forth all kinds of speculation. We have lately been jostled out of our comfortable delusion that time and space are the same over there as over here; they have been simply past, present, and future marching along at an even rate; and height, width, and breadth have been the unalterable containers of the universe.

Now, we are told by scientists familiar with Einstein's theories of time and space that both are flexible.

"We might compare our traditional idea of Time to a

rope that seems whole and unaltered as it passes through our world but is now frayed and insecure at each end far away from us," writes Mr. Priestly. "But if it will no longer do for stars and atoms, it is still good enough for man. In other words, I believe that many scientists (perhaps most of them) cling all the more tenaciously to the classical concept of Time, so far as our life in this world is concerned, because it has been so successfully challenged in the application elsewhere, on the largest and smallest scales. They feel strongly that nobody must start picking at the middle of the rope, where it seems still to hold. This explains—though in my opinion it does not justify—the shouts of 'Bosh!' 'Not tested!' 'Not proved!' 'Mere coincidence!' that greet any appearance of parapsychology and ESP, precognition, and new theories of Time. I can imagine them crying to each other, with Yeats: *Things fall apart; the center cannot hold.*"

This is running a little ahead of us, but it demonstrates the occasional similarity of thinking between Priestly and Cayce. The former is concerned in his book with time as it relates to man's entire experience: his world of thought and dreams, his unexplained and unaccountable adventures beyond the five senses. He seems to arrive at the same conclusions suggested by Cayce, and even the imagery they use to describe time and space (because we must attach them to some material concept in order to work with them at all) is identical. He compares the idea of time here to a "rope"; Edgar Cayce speaks of the "skein of time and space."

Just as is this modern writer, Edgar Cayce was quite explicit on the two different kinds of time in our experience. Cayce indicated this in many references to these abstract ideas and said that actually there was *no* time and space, and that these terms are merely conveniences for us here in a three-dimensional plane. "Time and Space are the elements of man's own concept of the Infinite and are not realities as would be any bodily element in the earth . . ." he explained.

Time and space are moreover manifested in the vastness of the heavens, said Cayce. "This becomes hard to conceive in the finite mind; as does the finite mind fail to grasp the lack of, or *no*, time." He speaks of a certain date in history as being "as Time is counted now, or light years—day and night years." This is *our* way of counting time. Then he adds: "Not light years as . . . counted by astrology or astronomy, in the speed or the reflection of a ray of light . . ." This is seemingly a reference to the new concept of Time which is "frayed and insecure at each end," as Priestly describes it.

Just as Priestly has surmised, the mysteries of ESP, including precognition, can be better studied by way of grappling with the nature of time and space, as we find in Cayce's statements. Priestly tells of a "torrent of correspondence" which he received in response to an appeal once on television to the public for letters of personal experience with ESP. He states, "Comparatively few of them were conerned with any theory of Time, even though they might have read—or tried to read—Dunne. They believed in their experience—and in some instances this might go back half a century, my correspondents being of all ages between eighteen and the eightys—and so they were glad to pass it on. . . .

"The prevailing notion of Time was not then challenged. Our contemporary idea of ourselves was not questioned. Something odd had happened, that was all; it could not be fitted into the accepted pattern, so it was ignored. Nobody, man or woman, in this great middle range pointed out that if one, just one, precognitive dream could be accepted as something more than a coincidence—bang goes our conventional idea of Time!"

This is a familiar reaction to these concepts. We are too close to our own experience of life to be able to be objective and to see the larger issues.

But if most people do not relate their subjective perception to the problems of time, Priestly brings to us the thoughts of several great minds who have. One chapter is devoted to the scientist's contribution to our understanding; another, to time as presented in fiction and drama, reflecting, of course, our many kinds of approaches to time in real life. He presents the theories of J.W. Dunne, who described in *An Experiment with Time* the dreams he had which set him to puzzling about time. Led into this brilliant scientist's maze of reasoning, we see in it, here and there, some thoughts comparable to Cayce's. But Edgar Cayce

185

said in a few words what most scientists must take hundreds of words to say, and he said it with authority.

Priestly also discussed the Esoteric school, where we feel more at ease. Here is reviewed the influence of Ouspensky in *Tertium Organum* and his other works. He describes the "Work" of Gurdjieff and Ouspensky as "far removed from the usual soft and sentimental doctrine of Higher Thought, Theosophy, and the rest: it is hard, demanding, grimly unsentimental."

In his chapter on "Time and Ancient Man," Priestly points out that primitive man had ideas of time different from ours today. Modern man feels his life being "ticked away" by an inescapable beat; primitive man, such as the Australian aborigine, has a more meaningful rapport with time. "Their myths relate the deeds of great ancestors or heroes," says Priestly. Quoting A.P. Elkin's *The Australian Aborigines,* he says that to these people, the "past" belongs "to that same sacred time of the spirit homes—it is also present. The usual term that they use for the past creative period also means 'dreaming'; their myths are about the eternal dream time. . . . The time to which they [the myths] refer partakes of the nature of dreaming; as in the case of the latter, past, present, and future are, in a sense, coexistent—they are aspects of the one reality."

Priestly then cites other ancient cultures in which time was undifferentiated, and decries by contrast our own culture with its absorption in technology, materiality, and the mechanical living which becomes meaningless for us. Picturing the "eternal dream time" of the primitive man, with his ritual and myths, heroes, and gods, he says that Elkins considers this the life in which any human being really finds his place in society and in nature, whether primitive or civilized, and in which he is brought in touch with the invisible things of the past, present, and future.' From it, "men obtain courage and strength, but not if they desecrate or neglect the sites, break the succession of initiates, forget the myths, and omit the rites, all of which results in the loss of an anchor in the past, a source of strength, and a sense of direction for the future."

Modern man yearns for this kind of relationship to time, says Priestly. We are "haunted" by the various kinds of

186

similar relationships enjoyed by the ancient Egyptians, Mesopotamians, East Indians. Even the Greeks, he states, had a different and more inclusive viewpoint. They imagined time to be moving in a circle in which things repeat themselves.

It is in the arts rather than in formal scientific reasoning, Priestly finds, that modern man has more easily managed to keep, or perhaps only lately to discover, his new understanding of time. "Erich Kahler, who was enthusiastically praised by Thomas Mann and Einstein, is not primarily concerned with Time in his wide-ranging study of modern man, *The Tower and the Abyss*. But he observes, in his notes on various great modern poets, 'a profound feeling of contraction not only of space but of time—a gathering of all times and their contents, of our entire existence in one sublime moment, a concentration which is almost equivalent to an abolition of time.' And in his later examination of the 'stream of consciousness' techniques so characteristic of modern fiction, he turns to Time once more. These new techniques, he tells us, having broken through the bottom of our consciousness, have likewise 'cracked the supposedly solid foundation of chronological time. A new time begins to germinate within time, the time of inner experience within the time of outer happenings. This new time has no definite limits—the depths into which it expands are practically infinite. It cannot be measured by means of chronological time.' "

Among the many ways to observe time is through the phenomenon of dreams, as Priestly points out.

In dreams, time seems to have no existence. It is not its passage which occupies us, but the reality of the message. Nor is space given a rational treatment. It is as if the mind no longer needed to be bound by time and space, but could see in this state what is important.

If we deal then with time as an artist does, we are freed from the bonds of definite, conventional limitations, just as we are in dreams. If we are thus freed, we say, "This old man with the sad eyes lived in Time and Space for a while. But let me show you the eternal truth about him! He exists yesterday, today, and tomorrow, though his body decay and this canvas will not always be intact!"

If a writer wishes to bring home to his reader the impact of an incident upon one of his characters, he uses the "flashback" technique which carries the reader to another scene in the story, to juxtapose events not as they occurred in historic time, but for the truth as it exists eternally.

And so, Priestly was concerned with the way time has changed for us since the theories of Einstein were introduced. He sees this new view (as opposed to the old, Newtonian concept,) as related to the problems of understanding precognition, ESP, dreams. He finds that Einstein's theory, however, "gives no allowance for any mechanism for reaching into the future. Past and future are very clearly separated in the relativistic models—in a sense more clearly than in previous views."

In a discussion with a high-ranking professor of physics, Priestly learned that "the theory of relativity, and particularly Minkowski's contribution to it, led people to adopt a certain attitude to time. (Minkowski said something like 'From now on space and time will lose their independence, and only their union will be real.') This tended to encourage people to think of space-time as ultimate reality which we experience section by section. This has some resemblance to Dunne's theory, but the latter assumes that all events, both past and future, are *there*. . . ."

More and more like Cayce!

In general, Edgar Cayce's readings tend to confirm all that the scientists, the modern writers, artists, and scholars are thinking these days about time and space being one and the same, and yet different "at both ends of the rope." But Cayce carries this further, and helps us to understand the riddle which Priestly poses for us, "What is the future?" The answers lie in the confirmation of quite another idea that has long been with us in our Judaic-Christian heritage and is found in the Old Testament. It is, we think, the "book of remembrance" referred to in Malachi 3:16, and is the "data . . . between Time and Space" which we quoted from the readings at the beginning of this chapter.

It is, said Cayce, this "book of remembrance," the record of all that happens in time and space, which he "read." It may be read, he added, by anyone sufficiently gifted to do so.

Would you believe that everything in history, everything that is happening on earth today, is being recorded on an etheric television screen, sound and all?

Remember, television and radio waves have always existed in the ether, and that man has merely *discovered* them, not created them! All man has done is to find mechanical ways to use them for his benefit, and this is, of course, remarkable in itself. But they have been there all along, down the centuries and eons of time: the *recorders* of the universe!

A popular television program illustrates this—in it, people are televised and recorded all unaware and unrehearsed.

We are, to be candid, on record—what Cayce calls the "Akashic Records."

The records of what a person does and thinks are thus forever preserved. It was this record which Cayce said he was able to "read" clairvoyantly. It is, he added, a scientific fact, the laws of which are possible to discover and which will be discovered one day.

This record is called in the readings at various times, "The Akashic Records," "The Book of Life," and "God's Book of Remembrance." It is, he said, "the record that the individual entity itself writes upon the skein of Time and Space, through Patience, and is opened when self has attuned to the Infinite, and may be read by those attuning to that consciousness."

"For the light moves on in Time, in Space" is given further, "and upon that skein between them are the records written by each soul in its activity through eternity—through its awareness—not only in matter, but in thought in whatever realm the entity builds for itself in its experience, in its journey, in its activity."

These records are made in relation to our environment, our heredity, and according to our ideals. Thus not only the factual record, but an evaluation of the record is there. When the Akashic records are "read," these factors of environment, heredity and ideals are taken into consideration.

It is from the Akashic Records that knowledge of the future is possible. This is because, said Cayce, all time is one: past, present, future. "Do not confuse present and past—they are one, if the entity, the soul, will make itself attuned to the whole purpose of Creative Energies and forces that manifest themselves in the activities of the individual.

The fourth dimension in Einstein's treatment of the "space-time continuum" was spoken of by Cayce, who described the fourth dimension as "an idea"—or an idea is the best we can comprehend of the fourth dimension! Therefore, of course, it cannot be envisioned, but we have a clue to what it is like in other words of Cayce's which describe the records as being "upon the esoteric, or etheric, or Akashic forces, as they go along upon the wheels of Time, the wings of Time, or in whatever dimension we may signify as a matter of its momentum or movement."

The Akashic Records began, said Cayce, with Creation. "For, in that creation in which souls of men were given the opportunity to become aware of those forces without themselves, when Time and Space began, there was given that incentive for each entity, each soul, in whatever environment it might be, to make a manifestation of its (the entity's) awareness of its relationships to the Creative Forces, or God . . .

"Thus, irrespective of what the entity has done or may do, there is *within itself* the records of what it has done, upon the skein of Time and Space." (Author's italics.)

Describing creation in another reading, Cayce tells of the appearance of matter, space, time. He gave a special place to patience, for he said that it was "in Patience" that all the rest of creation has evolved!

"Even being God ain't no bed of roses!" God says in the play *Green Pastures*. The line serves to tell us something of the patience that is required even of the Almighty in dealing with creation!

Cayce said, in analyzing self, the entity finds itself body, mind, and soul that answers in the three-dimensional plane to the Godhead—Father, Son, Holy Spirit. God moved, the Spirit came into activity. In the moving it brought Light, and then chaos. In this Light came Creation of that which in the earth came to be matter; in the spheres about the

190

earth, Space and Time; and in Patience it has evolved through those activities until there are the heavens and all the constellations, the stars, the universe as it is known—or sought to be known by individual soul-entities in the material plane.

"Then came into the earth materiality through the Spirit pushing itself into matter. Spirit was individualized and then became what we recognize in one another as individual entities. Spirit that uses matter, that uses every influence in the earth's environment, for the glory of the Creative Forces, partakes of, and is a part of, the universal consciousness.

"As the entity, an individual, then applies, it becomes aware—through Patience, through Time, through Space —of its relationship to the Godhead—Father, Son, Holy Spirit. In self it finds body, mind, soul. As the Son is the builder, so is the mind the builder in the individual."

One day, perhaps the mechanical means will be discovered which will enable us to "tune in" to these records. This is possible, Cayce said, so that we will be able perhaps to tune in to the conversations of Socrates, or of Jesus, or the First Continental Congress! For these records are like radio waves which can be picked up from the ether, if we but know how to locate them.

But as we learn to apply ourselves to finding our relationship to the Godhead, as the above reading instructs us, and to understand and use our minds to the fullest extent, even such a mechanical device for communication with God will become unnecessary. However, as not all of us will be able to "tune in" psychically, the invention of a "universal radio" will be perhaps as important to us as television is now. We don't all develop at the same pace, as Cayce reminded us, and some will even prefer the "cosmic sets" as being more "sceintific," more accurate receivers than mental ones.

Probably, we will develop our mental capacities—that is, our reasoning and thinking abilities—right along with the psychic ones. This is what Cayce said was true of the Atlanteans. Therefore, we will be still highly individual in the use of mental powers. Prophecy, psychic healing, creative and artistic ability, will all likely be commonplace everywhere, and will be as "normal" as intellectual attributes. The ideal will conceivably be a combination of all of these in each person!

Time and the Psyche

Not only can precognition be explained against the formula of Time, Space and Patience, but so, too, can intuition, perception beyond mere factual knowledge, telepathy, teleportation. Priestly tells of his own experience in still another realm of the mind: creativity. He wrote, he says, several plays within a very short time, hardly laboring over them at all, and yet they were well-written and pleasing to him and others. He felt that he was not really doing the writing, but that there was a selflessness involved.

This is a joyous experience for a creative person, and when he finds he has "dashed off" some excellent work, he is as amazed as anyone else that this happened to him!

Thus, artists, composers, writers, poets—all, in fact, who lend themselves to creative endeavor—partake of this freedom from conventional time, as do those gifted in psychic ability.

"In spite of this astounding speed of composition," writes Priestly, "it did not occur to me then that any Time element was involved. With Jung's theories in mind, I felt that the hard work in this apparently effortless playwriting had somehow been done in and by the unconscious, which had then broken through and taken charge and used my conscious mind simply as a transcribing instrument. So it did not occur to me that there was any Time element in this almost magical creation—for however modest its results may have been in terms of world drama, it was almost magical to me.

"But now I see that we cannot rule out Time, which has its own relation to the unconscious. We know that on one level the unconscious is capable of keeping an eye on chronological time for us, waking us if necessary at any hour we choose. But this is not its own time. It refuses to accept, when it is about its own business and not acting as an alarm clock, our whole idea of temporal succession. It's time is not ours, as Jung himself pointed out to me, some years later. . . ."

As we indicated in the chapter on the Pyramid Prophecies, a woman was told in a reading that her tomb was a part of the Hall of Records in Egypt, where there are thirty-two tablets with inscribed information. She asked how she might find the records and was told that she would be able to obtain them "mentally," even as far as interpreting them. "Seek through those (psychic) channels for guidance—as it is felt that it is needed," she was advised. This applied to her work in the Association, as well.

Once, Tom Sugrue asked Cayce how to go about describing an event he knew only at second hand, with but a few facts to guide him, in building a general picture of conditions in a story he was writing. "Use the imagination!" said Cayce.

Thus, we have two kinds of psychic perception suggested for these people, and they both demand a certain independence from time and space. The woman would have to defy the centuries of time that existed between the twentieth century A.D. and the eleventh century B.C., not to speak of the physical distance between herself here in the United States and the pyramid ruins of Egypt! Yet how else would she be able to obtain those records?

Tom Sugrue's problem, we would think, was similar. And yet, Cayce implied that the information they both received would be as accurate as though they had obtained it in materiality.

In using the imagination, in using our psychic intuition, we move around in infinity! Others were told to do the same, and a few more "Atlanteans," at least, were told that their activities in Egypt (or in other areas, but particularly in Egypt), were still a part of them and could be a meaningful influence in their present lives. They were stirred by these influences. If they were to go back to Egypt, they would be overtaken with old emotions—a kind of nostalgia?—that were engendered there.

One such person was an Egyptian who had built temples. "And if the entity but gazes upon those builded—by self, even, or under self's supervision—there comes the feeling of awe in the present; not only from that those meant to to the entity during the experience, but from the constant harking—mentally, spiritually, to those tenets through the experience. . . ."

Another person was termed to be "the eighth from
193

Adam," who, according to the Bible, was Methuselah. We are given that he lived "in the days of the exodus, and the periods of understanding through those activities." He had traveled from Chaldea, but spent time studying the records that were being compiled at that time "for the seeker to know his relationships to the past, the present, and the future, when counted from the material standpoint. And as the entity sought in those experiences to make Time and Space, as well as Patience, the realms that express the universality of the Force called God, so may this become in the present experience that in which the entity may excel—in giving that assurance to those who seek their closer understanding of the relationships one to another."

Now, this person (who was, by the way, the grandfather of Noah) was told that often "he may lose self in those things that are found there."

No Time, No Space

It is difficult to realize the magnitude of space, and furthermore, to understand that there actually is no time and no space. These are merely concepts, Cayce said, for our use in our limited condition. An interesting idea then is that if this is so, this would explain how we can go "back" in time or "cross" space, or look "ahead" into the future, for if these are but illusions, there are no barriers to our consciousness!

One person was told by Cayce that this was an explanation of how the effects of an event which happened in his childhood were being re-enacted years later. This man asked: "Did the fall I had, out of a swing when a child, hurting my head, cause an injury, causing a nervous condition all these years?"

Cayce replied: "This, of course, is—Remember that Life as a whole is one. If no Time or No Space—and these are elemental facts—then the effect of same is being re-enacted as it were into the body at present, but it is the general debilitation that is setting in. This may be a few weeks, it may be a few months; but these are beginning."

Cayce is saying here that the effect is "re-enacted," which means it must have been enacted at the time of the injury. And yet it is being re-enacted in time (or our illusion of time) because that's the way results are brought about in our three-dimensional world.

But in the realm of no-time, the result had already happened simultaneously with the accident. For "that as lived today is as tomorrow today, for today is tomorrow, tomorrow is today."

Cycles and Deadlines

There is a discipline in our dealing with time, however. For there are both cycles and deadlines, which work like our own concept of time: according to clocks and calendars. The ancients were aware of these cycles, as Priestly indicates. Cayce stated that time moves in cycles, and that much repeats itself. And so we find that although man has free will, he is also under the influence of these great circles. They are frightening, because one feels caught between the pincers of two points in time—one in the past, the other in the future. Having seen, for instance, that a certain type of event take place every twenty-five years, or every hundred years, or whatever, we find the next recurrence inevitable.

And the inevitable is what our free wills try to avoid!

In fact, nothing else in the study of time seems inevitable except the kind of prediction based on cycles; and even this, Cayce implies, can be modified by our wills.

But if we make the record in time, time, nevertheless, has power over us. There are, as we pointed out in "Destiny of Nations," cycles of milleniums, as was shown in the history of the Jews. We indicated the workings of the economic cycles for the world, which Cayce said occurred every twenty-four or twenty-five years, as given in "People Rising." He also spoke of the seven-year cycle of the body, which, he said, renews itself completely during each.

A spectacular example of the manner in which the stars repeat their influence over long periods of time was given in the reading for a woman in 1941: "Unusual astrological aspects affecting every soul in the earth to 'think differently,' to 'have varied urges' in the next two weeks—April 29 through May 12. It has been over eight hundred years since such has been the urge. . . . Think of the darkness of the spiritual life as was enacted then, and see what is the experience through which so many souls are passing and we pass during this period in the relationships of man to man.

"Will ye as a Soldier of the Cross do thy part?"

Spring, 1941, found the world at war although America of course was not yet in it.

But what dark time comparable to the early days of World War II had existed eight hundred years before?

This was the time the Second Crusade failed, and Jerusalem fell to the Moslems! The date? 1147-49— or 794 years before 1941.

In a World Affairs reading given the same day, Cayce explained again that beginning April 29, 1941, the Sun, Moon, Jupiter, Uranus, and Venus would all be in one sign. "When last this occurred," he said, "the earth throughout was in turmoil, in strife."

He went on to say that sixteen hundred years before this present conflict, when the earth was under these signs, that the powers of light and darkness were clashing, just as at the time of the Crusades, and World War II. "As in those periods, so today—we find nation against nation, the powers of death, destruction, the wrecking of that which has been and is held near and dear to the hearts of those who have through one form or another set ideals."

To what third world event was this related? By 340 A.D. the Democracy of Rome had been replaced by oriental despotism, first under Diocletian and later under Constantine—sixteen hundred (and one) years before 1941!

It would seem that the combination of these five heavenly bodies does this earth no good.

Further study of these two readings given on the same day brings up the question of why Cayce treated these events as he did. The woman was given the time of the Moslem capture of Jerusalem; the group inquiring on World Affairs, the Fall of Rome.

Cayce was being appropriate, as usual. The woman had evidently been a part of the unsuccessful Second Crusade and stood to gain from that experience in this present life. The Fall of Rome was of special significance to World Affairs students.

It would seem that prophecy has a definite advantage in taking into consideration the cycles of time. Astrologers, of course, know the zodiac and predict from a purely calculated basis, knowing the stars' influences and how they bear on individuals and nations.

Analyzing every hidden thought or intuitional insight, as Priestly does throughout his book, he gives us some valuable thoughts on the cycles of time as the East Indians believe they are. He is dismayed by their overwhelming view of time, which dwarfs our everyday attempts to live in the here and now. He describes the "Indian Time Trick: . . . an old emaciated Indian magically appears in your office. He begins by pointing out that a single daytime of Brahma lasts 4,320,000,000 of your years . . . and how the mahayuga consists of four ages each of them longer than your historical records, and that one thousand mahayugas constitute a kalpa, and that fourteen kalpas make up one manvantara. . . ."

Certain periods in time are good, others not so good, whether a cycle can be discerned or not. Such a time was the year 1936, when the Spanish War flared, Stalin began his mass purges, and Hitler marched into the Rhineland.

But the most interesting year, we think, was 1932, when Edgar Cayce made many important predictions for this century—perhaps his most important, from a world standpoint. At the same time, the events of that year had great bearing on those predictions.

Some of the events of 1932 were:

As given in the Cayce readings, the New Age was officially "begun."

The Pyramid Prophecies were given and interpreted by Edgar Cayce.

The Depression was in its worst year.

Cayce made an interesting prediction on the future understanding of evolution.

Cayce predicted earth changes, wars, and political upheavals, to begin 1936.

Wilson's role as peace-maker was made clear.

Cayce declared Russia's future religious development to be the hope of the world.

Related to these were several events which by themselves do not seem significant, but when taken in this context, point to a general stirring in the world to the unseen influences arising. Probably much more could be told, but those that pertain to world conditions are very relevant here.

In 1932 many areas of human endeavor revealed a concern for earthquakes, volcanoes, and their effects—and man's dominion in the earth! The Coast and Geodetic Survey began to record earth motions in the western United States. That same year, geologist Ugo Mondello stated that new lands would probably rise "one day" in the South Atlantic. James Henry Breasted gave the world his scholarly insight into the unity of "the works of nature and the works of man"—at the same time that Cayce was saying that man's relationships to his fellowman, or his spiritual life "oft keep many a city and many a land intact."

What a time to begin the New Age! At the bottom of the barrel, we *had* to start improving. Another decade and we had landed ourselves in another world war. But in 1950 we began a new period symbolized in the Pyramid Prophecies as "the King's Chamber." The meaning of this, said Cayce, was "the joy, the buoyance" promised for this new age.

If there are cycles and deadlines, their existence is for our benefit, we think. Time, Cayce said, was relative, often, but for some matters he was quite specific. When he predicted that China would one day be the "cradle of Christianity" he added that it was "far off as man counts time, but only a day in the heart of God." In the reading on Jesus' childhood and training, he said that the Master was in Egypt for five years "as you count time." These brief phrases encountered here and there emphasize the dual nature of time and affirm that there is another way of viewing it.

This was quite distinct, however, from the definite deadlines he gave, the towering beacon of them all being the year 1998 A.D. All along, there have been predictions that certain years would bring certain events. Such a year was 1958 when the principles of electromagnetism were to be discovered, and they were! Yet, in the same year the records of the Great Pyramid were to have been uncovered, but because of man's unreadiness for this, it did not come about. Destiny is influenced by man's will, but there is a time when it is rendered irreversible, by his will. It is even left to man his "time to be born, to die." Certain times were allotted for the influx of Atlanteans, and the year 1943 was

198

the year after which no one would be born who had not heard "The Lord He is God."

The Great Pyramid as a Monument of Time

The Great Pyramid utilizes space mathematically to interpret time.

If the Hall of Records contained the written past, present, future of man in the earth, why was it necessary to record this in stone? The Pyramid of Gizeh is this record expressed in terms of space, as well as in terms of time. There is need to identify time with space. Without the Pyramid, the full significance of the Prophecies would be lost to us. The Pyramid would appear to teach, even by an imaginary walk down its corridor and into the different chambers, a lesson in the unity of time-space.

So, too, the Sphinx was built to make space articulate, its location being in deliberate relationship to the rays of the sun falling in a certain way. "As the sun rises from the waters," said Cayce, "the line of the shadow (or light) falls between the paws of the Sphinx."

Then, the Pyramid and the Sphinx are studies in infinity. It is the Pyramid, however, which represents, embodies the ideal of time as no other structure on earth. Its secret is to be revealed "when the time has been fulfilled." Its very position in the center of the earth, as Cayce said, further clarifies for us the importance of space in presenting its message of, in, for all time. It occupies space in a special way, and from the center of the earth, its relationship to the universe is made plain by a mystical affinity to the stars. "At the correct time, accurate imaginary lines can be drawn from the opening of the Great Pyramid to the second star in the Little Dipper, called Polaris or the North Star. . . ."

"Time, Space, and Patience"

The sad part is that the world could not make better use of the Cayce data and has had to wait for the future to take it by the scruff of the neck and drag it into the light. Things would have been easier, it seems, if the world had had Cayce's ideas to work with.

Prophecy about what man would do, though, was qualified often and took into consideration the human will, many times. Gathering from what the readings said about future events he predicted, it would seem that *all* of these events were orignated in the *wills* of individuals in times past, and were only now becoming predictable without further room for change. He spoke of "tendencies in the hearts and souls of men" as being such that upheavals may be brought about.

"Our decisions undeniably influence the course of future events," said Dr. von Braun. This is attested to by Cayce, who had much to say about decisions and their effects on our future destiny.

One such study in decisions involves a time span of nine hundred years, between decisions made and the time of reckoning with them. And, although it bridges a perfectly measurable length of time as we understand it in the old way, the time measured by calendars and clocks, it tends to give a picture, too, of the way time is condensed for us in living out many lives. For, in reincarnating, we pick up where we left off in the last life, or perhaps we take up a karmic debt after many lives—but the continuity of cause and effect is there like a river flowing along.

Marcia Delgado wrote Edgar Cayce that she "sought advice dealing with the problems and conditions which have come about as the result of the decision made January 1, 1944."

Cayce began her reading with: "These are decisions which were made first in December, 1020!"

Marcia was reminded of her decisions made in December, 1020, in connection with her present husband. Her relationship with him had not been a happy one, we assume, nor the decision altogether wise, or there would be no painful repercussions from it now.

"In, then, the undertakings of the problems of today, each of these will be found to be part of that to which ye attempt to attain. Not merely the experiences of the moment, for that which happened in time, years ago, is today bearing fruit. Are ye gathering it ripe, or are you letting it destroy itself on the tree of life? Or are ye ignoring it altogether?"

The report reads that Marcia remained with her husband

and children, due to the counsel she received in this reading, and thus rectified a wrong decision of the past with a right one in the present. The decision was obviously not easy, for she soon had a nervous breakdown. After a brief period of hospitalization, however, she returned home to fulfill those eleventh-century decisions.

How can we know when we are making the right decisions? "By the listening within. . . . For the answer to every problem, the answer to know His way, is ever within," Cayce answered.

The inner self is a part of the Infinite, while the self-will or personality (whch may lead us astray) is ever at war with the infinite "for the lack of what may be called stamina, faith, patience. . . ."

Actually, however, we are living the past, present, and future all at one time, said Cayce. Our lives are divided into "lives" for our own convenience, only: all time is one and all life is one.

Earlier in this chapter, we had a hint as to how this works in the example of the man who fell in childhood and was suffering from after-effects years later. This was a natural consequence of the fall, of course, but there is another quality of time at work which is apparently the secret of cause and effect zeroing in so accurately on our lives, in every circumstance. How is it that we meet an old enemy of the past, or a dear friend, or some other important person in our lives, in a chance meeting? How is it that we find ourselves involved in accidents, or financial straits, or an emotional problem that seemingly has no justification in this life?

According to Cayce, the debilitation going on in the man's body was being *re-enacted* because it had occurred already! In this is the key to the law of karma. "Do unto others as you would have them do unto you" is a wise maxim, because it take cognizance of this hidden characteristic of time. For as you treat others, you are setting up in that very moment the way you will be treated later: You are *enacting* your own fate.

Thus, the answer as to how we "happen" to meet our fate is explained in this example. Since there is no time or space, the cause of the fateful event and the event are simultaneous. This is perfection, we would think, in fitting the punishment to the crime, or the reward to the good deed.

"For the Law of the Lord is perfect: it converteth the soul . . ."

In explaining how groups, nations meet their joint destiny, it would seem that their individual thoughts and actions are just as effective in bringing about their joint destiny as their individual destiny. France, we recall, was paying a karmic debt during her occupation by Nazi Germany. America's joint prayers could have kept her out of war. Cayce spoke of the "sins" of each nation as though he were speaking of individual persons. Thus, on a smaller scale, karma is then possibly brought about in the event of small groups of people brought together in some common endeavor—or plight. An airplane crash, for instance, involving a group of people is not, by these rules, by chance. We might turn this to a happier example as found in the family, brought together by karmic debts to spend a lifetime making amends or just learning to get along.

Just as the universe could not have evolved without patience, neither can we. "Time, Space, Patience—through these you possess your souls" said Cayce. We begin to see the relationship which patience has to time and space. It takes patience to do unto others as we would have them do unto us. We don't in that moment experience the reward. Cause and effect are years apart.

In patience we "become aware of our souls, of our identity, of our being each a corpuscle, as it were, in the great body, in the heart, of our God. And He has not willed otherwise." In fact, it is out of our awareness of these concepts that it is possible for us to *know* the Infinite.

The records of what we have done in the past are found within ourselves and they are there for us to remember if we wish, for we have been promised "all things to our remembrance."

Thus, if we are haunted, as Priestly suggests, by our primitive experience with time and space, we might be prompted to study these ideas for their value in the inner life. Not that we would go backward into a primitive expression of these values, denouncing all of civilization's achievements, but that we might re-examine our identity as a small part of a great Being and what this means to us as "children of God."

The ESP of which we hear so much these days can be seen to belong both to the primitive culture and to the most advanced, as shown in the Atlantean "myth" we have presented here. Or in a Peter Hurkos, or a Jeane Dixon. In another realm, there is the mysticism of Christianity and of Judaism, and in religious circles, ESP is being investigated, we are told, with great interest. Mystics of every kind have access to the world of the paranormal, and have reportedly practiced out-of-the-body travel, thought transference, soul memory.

For all, Edgar Cayce advocated that character development should precede ESP, and as one grows in virtue—in patience—one will receive these gifts as a natural result.

He advised that in all of our seeking in these strange paths, that we take on the Christ Consciousness for protection and guidance. For above all else, the highest use of ESP is to "know ourselves to be His."

"Time never was when there was not a Christ and not a Christ Consciousness," Cayce declared.

Contrary to theological thinking, the Christ has existed in all Eternity because it is of Spirit. Jesus, the man, took on the Christ Spirit. He lived in a temporal body, subject to physical laws, but was able to transform its atomic structure when He ascended into Heaven.

"And, as has been given, again the time draws near when there shall be seen and known among men, in many places, the manifestations of such forces in the material world. For 'As ye have seen Him go, so will He return again.' "

One seeker, puzzled about many things concerning the Christ, was told: "Oft, to be sure, it has come to thine own consciousness, how could, how *could* He be in Heaven, in earth, in this place or that place, and be aware of an individual and at the same moment or same time be aware of that same presence in places miles, yea, leagues and leagues apart?

"Then, in all, through all, is the permeating influence of the Christ Consciousness."

In another reading Cayce said: "Who of the whole peoples of that city that His Temple of Jehovah had been sat in, looked upon the King on the Cross and thought or felt that there would come the day when His words, even, 'My peace I give unto you' would change the whole world, and that Time, even, would be counted from that death, that birth?"

And in still another, "What is the water of life? What is this that the Spirit and the Bride, or the Spirit and the Lamb, say to come and take of freely? Patience, Time Space! That we may know ourselves to be His; that our spirits, our souls, bear witness in the things that we do in which we bear witness of Him."

Just as Jesus dealt with the physical man, so, we are beginning to suspect, God is dealing with the physical heavens and earth. He is renewing them just as Jesus was able to regenerate the flesh. The body and the earth are, after all, made of the same stuff. If a new body, why not a new earth? Literally!

Then, the earth changes predicted for us were to be a very physical disturbance, according to Cayce, but the physical change will be due to the "desires, the purposes, the aims" of people everywhere. This will bring about a "new vision," a "new comprehension." "Can the mind of man comprehend no desire of sin, no purpose but that the glory of the Son may be manifested in his life? Is this not a new heaven, a new earth? For the former things would have passed away. . . ."

Why hasn't God done this long ago? Because, said Edgar Cayce, this is a joint project—the heavens and the earth are under the management of God and man. We are the ones who have held off new heaven and new earth and peace. "When there has been in the earth those groups that have sufficiently desired and sought peace, peace will begin. It must be within self."

Desire is the key. To attain peace, a new heaven, a new earth, we must desire them sufficiently, even as God desires them.

When we pray, "Thy kingdom come, thy will be done," we are saying the words that might carry this desire or that might remain empty words. Each Christian knows within when he says these words how much he really desires the kingdom and God's will be done.

This is the deepest prayer we know. It is the deepest and holiest of all Destiny. It sums up all other prophecy for all time, for it will be in earth as it is in Heaven. This is both prophecy and promise, as well as prayer.

"And yet, remember as He gave: Time is not yet complete, Time is not yet at hand. Why? The laws are set, love can only remove same. . . ."

THE A.R.E. TODAY

The Association for Research and Enlightenment, Inc., is a non-profit, open membership organization committed to spiritual growth, holistic healing, psychical research and its spiritual dimensions; and more specifically, to making practical use of the psychic readings of the late Edgar Cayce. Through nationwide programs, publications and study groups, A.R.E. offers all those interested, practical information and approaches for individual study and application to better understand and relate to themselves, to other people and to the universe. A.R.E. membership and outreach is concentrated in the United States with growing involvement throughout the world.

The headquarters at Virginia Beach, Virginia, include a library/conference center, administrative offices and publishing facilities, and are served by a beachfront motel. The library is one of the largest metaphysical, parapsychological libraries in the country. A.R.E. operates a bookstore, which also offers mail-order service and carries approximately 1,000 titles on nearly every subject related to spiritual growth, world religions, parapsychology and transpersonal psychology. A.R.E. serves its members through nationwide lecture programs, publications, a Braille library, a camp and an extensive Study Group Program.

The A.R.E. facilities, located at 67th Street and Atlantic Avenue, are open year-round. Visitors are always welcome and may write A.R.E., P.O. Box 595, Virginia Beach, VA 23451, for more information about the Association.